KB197301

Korean Grammar Palette for Beginners ❶

Written by   Miss Vicky (Hyojeong Shim)
Publisher   Kyudo Chung
Published by   Darakwon

First Published   2025. 2. 10

Editorial Planner   Hyukju Kwon, Taekwang Kim
Editor   Huchun Lee, Hyoeun Kim

Designed by   SINGTA Design
Illustrated by   Gentle mellow (www.instagram.com/gentlemellow/)
Proofread by   Anthony Kourakis

한 DARAKWON

Darakwon Bldg., 211 Munbal-ro, Paju-si, Gyeonggi-do, Republic of Korea 10881
Tel : 02-736-2031
Fax : 02-732-2037
(Marketing Dept. ext.:250~252, Editorial Dept. ext.: 291~296)

Copyright©2025, by Miss Vicky

All right reserved. No part of this publication may be reproduced, stored in a retrieval system,
or transmitted in any form or by any means, electronic, mechanical, photocopying or otherwise,
without the prior consent of the copyright owner. Refunds after purchase is possible only
according to the company regulations. Contact the telephone number above for any inquiry.
Consumer damages caused by loss, damage etc., can be compensated according to consumer
dispute resolution standards announced by the Korea Fair Trade Commission.
An incorrectly collated book will be exchanged.

ISBN 978-89-277-7452-5   13710

http://www.darakwon.co.kr
http://www.darakwonusa.com

Visit the Darakwon homepage to learn about our other publications and promotions
and to download the contents in MP3 format.

KOREAN GRAMMAR
PALETTE
for BEGINNERS 1

Written by **Miss Vicky**

  MP3 & YouTube Lecture

You can find more Korean lessons on the YouTube channel Korean with Miss Vicky!

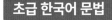 초급 한국어 문법

 DARAKWON

The Author's Message

안녕하세요!

This is Miss Vicky, the author of this book.
I'm so happy to present my new book,
Korean Grammar Palette for Beginners 1, which was written with
deep appreciation, affection, and care for Korean learners.

I chose the name Palette because I believe the language you speak
and write is, in many ways, a work of art—like a beautiful drawing. To
create these art pieces, you need colors to bring your blank canvas to
life. This book is designed to provide those colors—diverse grammar
concepts and expressions—so you can craft your own works of art in
Korean, both in speech and writing.

Everything covered in this book is essential yet practical, making
it useful not just for understanding the basics, but also for real-life
conversations and writing. I'm confident that this book will help
you build a strong foundation in Korean grammar, deepen your
understanding of the language, and improve your proficiency over
time. I encourage you to explore the content at your own pace without
the pressure to memorize everything word for word.

Last but certainly not least, I want to sincerely thank the editors
at the publishing house who worked tirelessly to coordinate the
design and layout, and to my YouTube subscribers
who continue to cheer me on every step of the way.

Thank you for making this book a part of your journey. 감사합니다.

Miss Vicky

Recommendation from a Student/Proofreader

I am extremely grateful for the opportunity to share
my experience learning with Miss Vicky, my Korean teacher
of four years, and share my thoughts on this exceptional textbook.

Before starting tutoring with Miss Vicky, I had a foundation
in Korean, but my progress was slow and often frustrating.
Under her expert guidance, my Korean skills improved
far beyond my expectations, and I gained the confidence
to navigate both formal and casual conversations
with ease. Her ability to explain even the most complex
grammar points with clarity and precision transformed
my learning experience.

This book is an invaluable resource for beginner learners.
It not only introduces essential Korean grammar points but also
explains them with incredible detail, supported by an abundance
of examples. What sets this textbook apart is its focus on real,
day-to-day spoken Korean, bridging the gap between
textbook knowledge and practical usage. Whether you are just
beginning your Korean language journey or looking to solidify
your understanding, this book will serve as a trusted guide
and companion.

Miss Vicky's passion for teaching and her deep understanding
of the Korean language shine through every page, making this
textbook a must-have for anyone eager to learn Korean.

Anthony Kourakis

How to use this book

This book is designed to guide you step by step, making your learning journey smooth, engaging, and enjoyable.

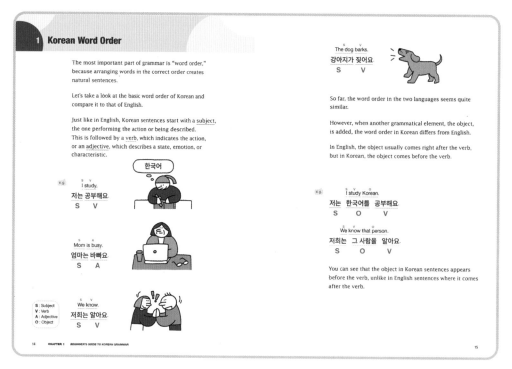

Each chapter starts with an explanation of a grammar concept, accompanied by example sentences to help you understand how it works in context. You'll also find **yellow tip boxes** that offer extra details or deeper insights where needed.

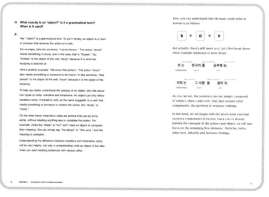

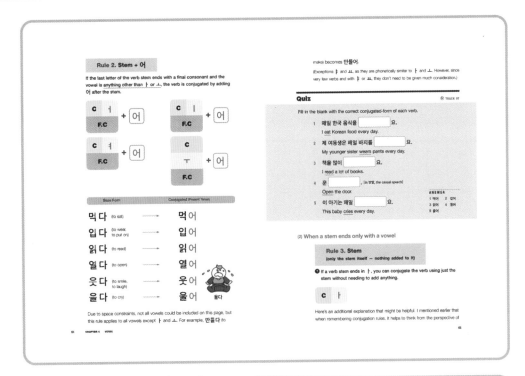

After exploring the explanations and examples, you can test your understanding with the **Practice** and **Quiz** sections, which are designed to help you apply what you've learned. Occasionally, you'll come across 꿀팁 **(honey tips)**—a fun Korean slang term for helpful advice—that will make your learning experience even smoother.

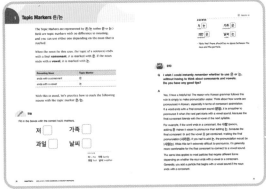

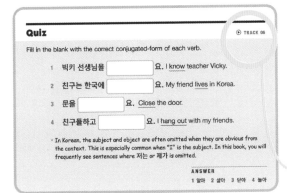

You can listen to **audio recordings** of the example sentences from the Practice and Quiz sections. A **QR code** on the book's flap provides quick and easy access to these audio files.

Audio Files

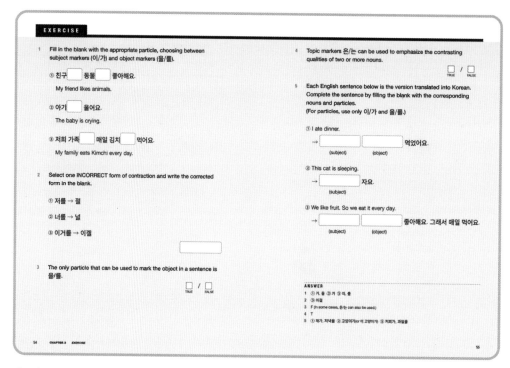

At the end of each chapter, there's an **Exercise** section where you can review and reinforce what you've learned. Additionally, you'll find a special section introducing aspects of Korean **culture**, **vocabulary**, or commonly used **phrases**, adding depth to your understanding of the language.

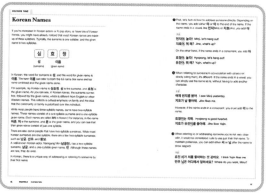

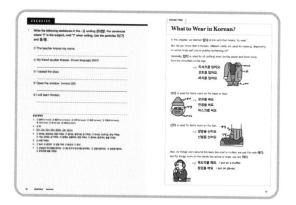

Appendix

Personal Pronouns in Korean

We've learned the Korean words for "I" and "You," but you may have noticed that "You," "He," "She," and "They" don't have a single universal equivalent in Korean. Unlike many other languages, Korean doesn't use fixed pronouns for these words in every context. In this appendix, we'll explore how personal pronouns work in Korean and the different ways they are used.

Personal pronouns in Korean work quite differently from English. Except for "I" and "We," there isn't a direct equivalent for "You," "He," "She," and "They." While we do have those pronouns, they are rarely used in daily conversation, making them not very practical. Instead, many alternative words are used to express each of those pronouns.

In this chapter, we'll explore different alternatives for "You," "He," "She," and "They," focusing on the most commonly used ones. Along the way, you'll also pick up new basic vocabulary and gain insights into aspects of Korean culture. Rather than approaching this chapter with the pressure to remember everything, feel free to think of it as reading for fun!

Lastly, the appendix includes practical information about Korean pronouns and an introduction to Korean titles, which play an essential role in communication and cultural context.

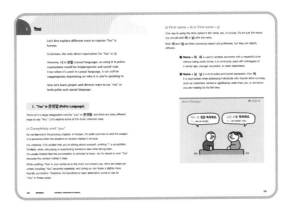

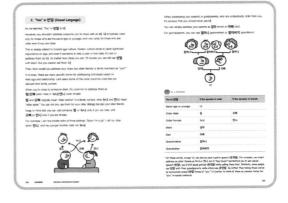

Table of Contents

CHAPTER 1

Beginner's Guide to Korean Grammar

This chapter is an overview of Korean Grammar and introduces essential terms that are useful to know when studying Korean.

Welcome to the first chapter of the book! With this chapter, I will walk you through the overview of how Korean grammar works.

I recommend using this chapter as a way to understand how Korean works overall, rather than trying to memorize everything. After reading this chapter, it will be much easier to follow and understand the rest of the chapters.

I also want to assure you that studying grammar doesn't have to be a rigid and boring process. In Korean, many parts that are referred to as grammar are actually just expressions. When creating sentences, you need vocabulary, right? You can think of grammar as a part of those vocabulary phrases.

Of course, grammar also includes "rules" in addition to merely being "expressions." There are many useful rules to learn in Korean grammar, especially for beginner learners. In this book, I will try my best to explain them in detail, in a way that's easy for you to understand. By learning these grammatical aspects, you will understand why the Korean language works the way it does and this understanding will help you retain the language more effectively as you advance to upper levels.

Now, without further ado, let's get started! Are you ready?

1 Korean Word Order

The most important part of grammar is "word order," because arranging words in the correct order creates natural sentences.

Let's take a look at the basic word order of Korean and compare it to that of English.

Just like in English, Korean sentences start with a <u>subject</u>, the one performing the action or being described.
This is followed by a <u>verb</u>, which indicates the action, or an <u>adjective</u>, which describes a state, emotion, or characteristic.

e.g.

S   V
I study.

저는 공부해요.
S   V

S   A
Mom is busy.

엄마는 바빠요.
S   A

S : Subject
V : Verb
A : Adjective
O : Object

S   V
We know.

저희는 알아요.
S   V

The dog barks.
강아지가 짖어요.
S   V

So far, the word order in the two languages seems quite similar.

However, when another grammatical element, the object, is added, the word order in Korean differs from English.

In English, the object usually comes right after the verb, but in Korean, the object comes before the verb.

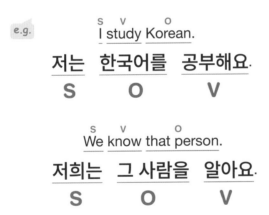

e.g.

I study Korean.
저는 한국어를 공부해요.
S   O   V

We know that person.
저희는 그 사람을 알아요.
S   O   V

You can see that the object in Korean sentences appears before the verb, unlike in English sentences where it comes after the verb.

Q   **What exactly is an "object?" Is it a grammatical term? When is it used?**

A

Yes, "object" is a grammatical term. To put it simply, an object is a noun or pronoun that receives the action of a verb.

For example, take the sentence: "I study Korean." The action "study" needs something to study, and in this case, that is "Korean." So, "Korean" is the object of the verb "study" because it is what the studying is directed at.

Here's another example: "We know that person." The action "know" also needs something or someone to be known. In this sentence, "that person" is the object of the verb "know" because it is the target of the knowing.

To help you better understand the concept of an object, let's talk about two types of verbs: transitive and intransitive. An object can only follow transitive verbs. A transitive verb, as the name suggests, is a verb that needs something or someone to receive the action, like "study" or "know."

On the other hand, intransitive verbs are actions that can be done alone, without needing anything else to complete the action. For example, verbs like "sleep" or "run" don't need an object to complete their meaning. You can simply say, "He sleeps" or "She runs," and the meaning is complete.

Understanding the difference between transitive and intransitive verbs will be very helpful, not only in understanding what an object is but also when you start creating sentences with various verbs.

Now, you can understand that the basic word order in Korean is as follows :

But actually, there's still more to it. Let's first break down these example sentences in more detail.

As you can see, the sentences are not simply composed of subject, object, and verb. They also include other components, like particles or sentence endings.

In this book, we will begin with the seven most essential sentence components in Korean. Since you've already learned the concepts of the subject and object, we will now focus on the remaining five elements : Particles, Verbs, Adjectives, Adverbs and Sentence Endings.

2 Essential Sentence Components

1. Particles 조사

A similar element in English would be prepositions like in, at, on, with, and for.

Particles cannot be used on their own, and they should be attached to **nouns**. (Some particles can also attach to adverbs.) Korean particles are also known as post-positions, because they are always placed <u>after</u> a noun.

e.g.
한국 <u>에</u> = <u>in</u> Korea
noun / particle

친구 <u>와</u> = <u>with</u> a friend
noun / particle

There are also some Korean particles that do not have equivalents in English. The most common examples are the topic marking particle, subject marking particle, and object marking particle. (The term "marking particle" is used interchangeably with "marker.")

As the names suggest, these particles mark nouns that function as the topic, subject, and object in a sentence. For example, in the previously mentioned sentence:

저 는   한국어 를   공부해요.
subject/topic   object

The particles 는 and 를 are the "topic marker" and "object marker," respectively.

Each particle has various functions and can be used differently depending on the context. We will learn more about these in detail in the chapter on particles.

2. Verbs 동사

Verbs mainly express actions.

In Korean, all verbs have a "base form," which is also referred to as the dictionary form. All base forms end with –다, and they consist of what is called the "stem" of the verb plus 다.

e.g. to study : 공부하다 (base form)

to know : 알다 (base form)

When verbs are used in sentences, however, the base form cannot be used as is; it must always be conjugated, either in past, present or future tense.

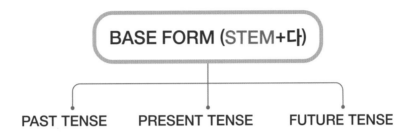

BASE FORM (STEM+다)

PAST TENSE   PRESENT TENSE   FUTURE TENSE

For example, the verb 공부하다 means "to study."
If you look at the example sentence:

저는 한국어를 공부해요. I study Korean.

you'll notice that 공부하다 has changed its form and is not used as it is.

(공부해 is the conjugated form of 공부하다 in the present tense.)

Similarly, the verb 알다 means "to know." In the example sentence:

저희는 그 사람을 알아요. We know that person.

you can see that the form of 알다 has also changed.

(알아 is the conjugated form of 알다 in the present tense.)

We will learn the specifics of the conjugation rules in the chapter on verbs.

3. Adjectives 형용사

e.g. I am happy.   저는 <u>행복해요</u>. (predicate / conjugated)

The weather <u>is hot</u>.   날씨가 <u>더워요</u>. (predicate / conjugated)

a <u>kind</u> person   **친절한** 사람 (modifier)

<u>long</u> hair   **긴** 머리 (modifier)

In each sentence and phrase, the words that function as adjectives are "am happy (**행복해**)", "is hot (**더워**)", "kind (**친절한**)" and "long (**긴**)." Adjectives are words that provide the information about the emotions, characteristics or state of a person or thing.

In Korean, adjectives are referred to as "descriptive verbs." This means that in a broad sense, adjectives are also considered verbs. Therefore, just like verbs, adjectives also have base forms and are conjugated into past, present, and future tenses.

In fact, in the first two example sentences, **행복해** is the conjugated form of the adjective **행복하다**, and **더워** is the conjugated form of **덥다**.

However, do you notice the difference in the last two example phrases?

친절한 사람 a kind person

긴 머리 long hair

Unlike the first two, these adjectives are placed before a noun. This happens when adjectives are in their modifier form, coming before the noun to directly modify it.

In Korean, adjectives have different forms depending on whether they are used as a predicate (hereafter referred to as "conjugated form") or as a modifier. Naturally, the grammatical rules for forming each are different, and you will learn these rules as you study adjectives.

Adjectives
- Conjugated Form (past, present, future)
- Modifier Form (formed by adding a corresponding suffix)

4. Adverbs 부사

Just now, we learned how adjectives function as "modifiers." In fact, adverbs also function as modifiers. So, what exactly does a modifier mean?

A modifier is a word, phrase, or clause that specifies or adds information to another word in a sentence. Both adjectives and adverbs are modifiers, but they have different uses.

Adjectives can only modify nouns, pronouns, or noun phrases. For example, in the phrase "a happy child," "happy" is an adjective that describes the noun "child."

In contrast, adverbs cannot modify nouns. Instead, they modify verbs, adjectives, or other adverbs. For example, in the sentence "She sings beautifully," "beautifully" is an adverb that describes how she sings.

There are many types of adverbs in Korean, and many of them come from adjectives, just like in English. For example, the adverb "beautifully" is formed by adding "ly" to the adjective "beautiful," and "slowly" is formed by adding "ly" to the adjective "slow." Similarly, Korean has specific suffixes that turn adjectives into adverbs, with the most common one being 게.

For example, you can take the adjective **아름답다** (to be beautiful) and add **게** to form the adverb **아름답게** (beautifully). Likewise, you can take the adjective **느리다** (to be slow) and add **게** to form the adverb **느리게** (slowly).

In addition to this, there are independent words that are classified as adverbs on their own, such as **매일** (every day) and **혼자** (alone).

A noun can also become an adverb when specific particles are attached to it. For example, **월요일에** (on Monday) is an adverbial phrase that provides information about time, and **학교에서** (at school) is one that provides information about place.

Depending on the type of adverb, where an adverb should be placed in a sentence can vary, but it invariably comes before the verb, and it is often placed immediately before the verb if it provides direct and specific information about the verb.

In fact, any adverb can be grammatically correct as long as it is placed anywhere before the verb. However, for adverbs that provide information about time or place, such as **월요일에** (on Monday) or **학교에서** (at school), it is a good rule of thumb, especially for beginners, to place them towards the beginning of the sentence, usually right after the subject.

Subject + (Time Adverb) + (Place Adverb) + Object + (Adverb) + Verb

e.g. 저는 평일에 학교에서 한국어를 열심히 배워요.

I on weekdays at school korean diligently learn.

(= I diligently learn Korean at school on weekdays.)

5. Sentence Endings 종결어미

So far in this book, you've learned that Korean sentences mostly end with a verb (or an adjective). But if you look closely at the verb part, you'll often see not just the verb itself but also a sentence ending attached to it.

저는   평일에   학교에서 한국어를   열심히   배워요.

(verb + sentence ending)

There are various sentence endings in Korean. In addition to indicating that a sentence has ended, they can also add specific meanings, make the sentence sound politer, or even indicate whether the sentence is a question or a statement.

As you advance, you will gradually learn a lot of sentence endings with different meanings. At the beginner level, the most essential sentence endings are the polite endings –요 and –ㅂ/습니다, also known as the 존댓말 endings.

존댓말 (Polite Language) vs. 반말 (Casual Language)

존댓말 literally means "treat-with-respect speech" and is referred to in English as either "polite language" or "formal language." It is used when speaking to anyone you want to be polite and show respect to. When meeting someone for the first time, it is customary to start the conversation in 존댓말.

반말 literally means half speech, which means that it is not a fully formal language. It is referred to in English as either "casual language" or "informal language" and is mainly used with people who you are close to, such as your family members, friends, or even someone who's much younger than you, like a little kid.

존댓말 and 반말 are mainly distinguished by the use of sentence endings, which are essential in 존댓말 to indicate respect. 존댓말 sentence endings are mainly divided into two types :

❶ –요

> e.g. 한국어를 배워요. I learn Korean.
>
> 고마워요. Thank you.

❷ –ㅂ/습니다 : This ending feels more formal than 요 and is often referred to as the "formal polite ending."

> e.g. 한국어를 배웁니다. I learn Korean.
>
> 고맙습니다. Thank you.

For 반말, there is no specific sentence ending, and you can simply end the sentence without adding any additional ending. (Some sentence endings have different forms for 존댓말 and 반말, but this is not something you need to worry about for now.)

In this book, most of the example sentences and exercises will be in 존댓말, specifically using the -요 ending. This is because 반말 is relatively easy to learn since you don't need to add any endings. Also, it's common to use 존댓말 when meeting people for the first time, and you need to be comfortable using polite language in the initial phase of interactions with Koreans.

You will also get to practice making sentences with the -ㅂ/습니다 ending in a separate chapter, so while studying with this book, you will get plenty of practice with both 존댓말 forms.

1   Arrange the following sentence elements in the correct order for Korean.

Subject   Verb   Object

_____

2   Select the correct one in the parentheses.

Korean particles are placed right (before / after) (nouns / verbs).

3   Below are the examples of the base form of verbs. Write the grammatical terms for the underlined part.

알<u>다</u>   배우<u>다</u>   공부하<u>다</u>

_____

4   Check whether the following adjectives function as conjugated forms (predicates) or as modifiers.

① <u>행복한</u> 사람   (conjugated / modifier)

② 머리가 <u>길어</u>요.   (conjugated / modifier)

③ <u>더운</u> 날씨   (conjugated / modifier)

④ 선생님은 <u>친절해</u>요.   (conjugated / modifier)

5 Write the grammatical term for each <u>underlined</u> element.

subject object verb adjective particle adverb sentence ending

I	on the weekend	delicious	food	a lot	eat
저<u>는</u>	주말<u>에</u>	<u>맛있는</u>	<u>음식</u>을	<u>많이</u>	<u>먹어</u> <u>요</u>.

[   ] [   ] [   ] [   ] [   ] [   ][   ]

6 All of the sentences below mean "I learn Korean." Check whether each sentence is in 반말 or 존댓말.

① 나는 한국어를 배워.　　　　(반말 / 존댓말)

② 저는 한국어를 배워요.　　　(반말 / 존댓말)

③ 저는 한국어를 배웁니다.　　(반말 / 존댓말)

ANSWER

1 Subject – Object – Verb

2 after, nouns

3 stem

4 ① modifier (행복한 사람 : a happy person)

　　② conjugated (머리가 길어요 : the hair is long)

　　③ modifier (더운 날씨 : hot weather)

　　④ conjugated (선생님은 친절해요 : the teacher is kind)

5 subject, particle, adjective, object, adverb, verb, sentence ending

6 ① 반말 ② 존댓말 ③ 존댓말

CHAPTER 2

은/는 & 이/가
Topic Markers &
Subject Markers

In this chapter, we will learn how to use the topic markers and subject markers along with their subtle differences in meaning.

 From this chapter onward, you will find 꿀팁, 연습 and Quiz sections. 꿀팁 means "honey tip," and it's a fun slang term for a highly useful tip. 연습 means "practice." Make good use of these sections to review what you've learned right away. By doing so, you'll be able to work through the exercises at the end of each chapter with more confidence.

The first Korean particles we will learn are the Topic Marking Particle (also known as Topic Markers) and the Subject Marking Particle (also known as Subject Markers).

In the previous chapter, we learned what a subject is. Then, what exactly is a "topic" in a sentence?

A "topic" refers to the noun that the sentence is mainly about. You might wonder, isn't that the same as the subject? That is also correct. Many nouns that are the subject of a sentence are indeed the topic. However, this is not always the case. Sometimes, an object of a sentence can also be the topic.

Therefore, you can consider the topic as a broader term compared to the subject. In fact, determining what the topic of a sentence is depends entirely on the speaker. The noun that the speaker particularly wants to bring attention to becomes the topic, whether it's a subject or an object.

Topic markers and subject markers also have other usages beyond indicating the topic and subject in a sentence. Depending on which one you use, the nuance of the sentence can change, and sometimes the meaning can differ as well.

Before learning about these subtle differences in meaning, let's first focus on the basic usage of these particles.

The Topic Markers are represented by 은/는 (either 은 or 는.) Both are topic markers with no difference in meaning, and you can use either one depending on the noun that is marked.

When the noun (in this case, the topic of a sentence) ends with a final **consonant**, it is marked with 은. If the noun ends with a **vowel**, it is marked with 는.

Preceding Noun	Topic Marker
ends with a consonant	은
ends with a vowel	는

With this in mind, let's practice how to mark the following nouns with the topic marker 은/는.

 연습

Fill in the boxes with the correct topic markers.

저 ☐   가족 ☐

과일 ☐   날씨 ☐

VOCAB
저 I, me   가족 family
과일 fruit   날씨 weather

ANSWER

저 는
vowel

가족 은
consonant

과일 은
consonant

날씨 는
vowel

* Note that there should be no space between the noun and the particle.

 꿀팁!

Q I wish I could instantly remember whether to use 은 or 는, without having to think about consonants and vowels. Do you have any good tips?

A

Yes, I have a helpful tip! The reason why Korean grammar follows this rule is simply to make pronunciation easier. Think about how words are pronounced in Korean, especially in terms of consonant assimilation. If a word ends with a final consonant sound (받침), it is smoother to pronounce it when the next part starts with a vowel sound, because the final consonant blends with the vowel of the next syllable.

For example, if the word ends in a consonant, like 사람 (person), adding 은 makes it easier to pronounce than adding 는, because the final consonant ㅁ and the vowel 으 get combined, making the final pronunciation [사라믄]. If you had to add 는, the pronunciation would be [사람는]. While this isn't extremely difficult to pronounce, it's generally more comfortable for the final consonant to connect to a vowel sound.

The same idea applies to most particles that require different forms depending on whether the noun ends with a vowel or a consonant. Generally, you add a particle that begins with a vowel sound if the noun ends with a consonant.

2 Subject Markers 이/가

Subject markers are represented by 이/가. Just like with topic markers, whether to use 이 or 가 depends on what the preceding noun ends with.

Preceding Noun	Subject Marker
ends with a consonant	이
ends with a vowel	가

Now, let's practice how to mark the following nouns with the subject marker 이/가.

 연습

Fill in the boxes with the correct subject markers.

저 ☐   직업 ☐

친구 ☐   선생님 ☐

VOCAB
직업 job
친구 friend
선생님 teacher

▶ TRACK 02

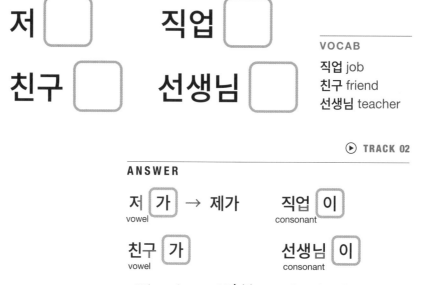

ANSWER

저 [가] → 제가   직업 [이]
vowel   consonant

친구 [가]   선생님 [이]
vowel   consonant

* When the word 저 (I) is combined with the subject marker 가, the final form changes to 제가. The form 저가 is not used.

Changes and Contractions

When 저 (I) is combined with the subject marker 가, it becomes 제가 instead of 저가. Besides this, there are other cases where forms change or where contraction forms are used interchangeably.

Let's learn about such variations and contractions.

1. Change of Form

There are a few nouns whose forms change when combined with a topic marker or subject marker. Here are the most common ones.

❶ 나 + 가 → 내가

   noun   subject marker

저 is "I" in the polite form (존댓말), whereas 나 also means "I" but in the casual form (반말). Just as 저 changes to 제가 when combined with 가, 나 changes to 내가 when combined with 가.

❷ 너 + 가 → 네가

   noun   subject marker

너 is "you" in 반말. When 너 is combined with 가, it changes to 네가*.

* The correct pronunciation of 네가 is literally [네가], but in everyday life, you will often hear people pronouncing it as [니가]. This pronunciation can be heard not only in daily conversations but also in K-dramas, movies, and song lyrics that reflect everyday Korean. 니가 is originally a dialectal pronunciation of 네가, and this change happens because 내가 (I) and 네가 (you) sound similar, and people unconsciously try to differentiate between the two by pronouncing 네가 as 니가. You might also hear people say 너가.

In short, the every-day pronunciation of 네가 can vary as 네가, 니가, or 너가, but the standard pronunciation is 네가, with 니가 being the most common in everyday use.

How do you say "you" in 존댓말?

One tricky part about Korean is that there is no fixed form of "you," and it all depends on whom you are talking to. This will be covered in more detail in the Appendix chapter at the end of the book, along with other personal pronouns (he, she, and they).

2. Contraction

❶ 거 + **가** → **게**

noun   subject marker

거 means "thing" and it's a less formal version of 것.

Although they are nouns, they cannot be used on their own and must always be used with a modifier or determiner.

- **이거** : this (as in, this one)
- **그거** : that (as in, that one)
- **저거** : that (as in, that one over there)

이거 + **가** → **이게**

noun   subject marker

그거 + **가** → **그게**

noun   subject marker

저거 + **가** → **저게**

noun   subject marker

❷ 저 + 는 → 저는, 전 (interchangeable)

    noun   topic marker

When 저 (I) and 는 are combined, both 저는 and its contraction 전 are interchangeable. The same goes for 나 and 너.

나 + 는 → 나는, 난 (interchangeable)

    noun   topic marker

너 + 는 → 너는, 넌 (interchangeable)

    noun   topic marker

The same goes for 이거, 그거 and 저거 when combined with 는.

이거 + 는 → 이거는, 이건 (interchangeable)

그거 + 는 → 그거는, 그건 (interchangeable)

저거 + 는 → 저거는, 저건 (interchangeable)

Quiz

▶ TRACK 03

Write the correct form.

1 나 + 가 → ⬚

2 너 + 가 → ⬚

3 이거 + 가 → ⬚

4 저 + 는 → ⬚

5 그거 + 는 → ⬚

ANSWER

1 내가 2 네가 3 이게
4 전/저는 5 그건/그거는

4 은/는 vs. 이/가 : Subtle Difference in Meanings

The example sentences in this section are meant to help you compare the different uses of 은/는 and 이/가. Even if they include grammar points you haven't learned yet, don't worry about fully understanding the Korean sentences. Just focus on the differences between 은/는 and 이/가.

If this section feels too difficult, you can always come back to it after finishing the rest of the book.

Other than 은/는 marking what's considered a "topic" in a sentence and 이/가 what's considered a "subject," the two particles can also convey different meanings and points of focus depending on the context.

The differences between 은/는 and 이/가 are famously tricky for students learning Korean. While it's possible to explain them to some extent, it's hard to provide an explanation that applies perfectly to every situation, given the wide range of conversational contexts.

For now, there's no need to learn about all the subtle differences. Also, this is something that you will gradually get the hang of by observing how native speakers use these particles in different contexts.

In this chapter, we'll focus on the key differences that are useful at a beginner level. You don't need to try to remember these differences. It's okay to simply read through them lightly for reference.

1. Centre (은/는) vs. Non-centre (이/가)

The noun that serves as the **focus** of the sentence is marked with 은/는.

On the other hand, the noun that is not necessarily the main focus is marked with **이/가**.

This distinction is the reason why 은/는 is often referred to as the **TOPIC** marking particle. It highlights the topic or theme that the sentence is focused on.

In contrast, **이/가** is typically used to mark the subject of the sentence without emphasizing it as the central point of discussion.

That's why it's common to attach 은/는 to a noun when introducing yourself, because when you are telling people about yourself, the focus of the sentence is usually on you.

> e.g. 제* 이름은 은지예요. My name is Eunji.
>
> 저는 학생이에요. I am a student.
>
> 저는 서울에 살아요. I live in Seoul.
>
> 저는 똑똑해요. I'm smart.

> * In Korean, "my" is expressed as 저의 or 제. The particle 의 is a possessive marker that can be attached to any noun to indicate possession. 저의 is commonly shortened to 제 in everyday speech. In casual speech, you can use 나의 or 내.

Likewise, when your intention is to talk about someone (or something) else and provide information about them, you typically put 은/는 because the focus of the sentence is on them.

> e.g. 엄마는 한국 사람이에요. My mom is Korean.
>
> 한국은 아름다워요. Korea is beautiful.

 꿀팁!

If you're looking for an English expression similar to 은/는, you might think of phrases like "as for" or "when it comes to," as they both highlight the noun in focus. However, it's important to remember that they're not exact equivalents. This is because taking every sentence with 은/는 as "as for" or "when it comes to" can often sound awkward, and in many cases, 은/는 doesn't emphasize the focus as strongly as those English phrases do.

When learning Korean, it's a good idea to be mindful about trying to find the exact equivalent in English. The two languages have their own unique ways of expressing ideas, shaped by different cultures and thought processes, so it's best to embrace those differences as you learn.

Now, let's take a look at a sentence where 이/가 is used. What exactly does it mean when the noun isn't necessarily the focus of a sentence?

> *e.g.* A 부산에 또 놀러 와. Come visit Busan again.
>
> B 제가 서울에 살아요. 그래서 자주 못 와요.
>
> I live in Seoul, so I can't come often.

The phrase "I live in Seoul." is not used as general information about myself, but rather as an explanation or reason for the sentence that follows. So the focus is more on the fact that "I **live in Seoul.**" instead of the fact that "<u>I</u> live in Seoul." That's why using 이/가 would feel more natural in this context.

2. Noun is General vs. Specific

은/는 is used when the noun represents something general or when you're stating universal facts about it.

On the other hand, 이/가 is used when the noun is specific or when you're referring to it in a particular situation, example, or context.

e.g.

- 아기는 울어요.
  Babies cry. (a general, universal fact about babies)

- 아기가* 울어요.
  The baby cries.
  (a specific baby in a particular time or circumstance)

* 아기(baby) can be made more specific by adding modifiers such as 이 (this), 저 (that), or 지수의 (Jisu's), but often the 이/가 particle alone is enough to indicate the specific baby you are referring to, especially when it's clear from the context or situation. You can choose to include or omit the specific modifier, depending on whether the context makes it clear.

Q So, if I want to give general information about a specific baby, can I just say, "이 아기는 울어요" (This baby cries)?

A

Yes, that's correct! When you want to describe a general characteristic of 이 아기(this baby), you can use the topic marker 는.

However, the sentence 이 아기는 울어요 is something people wouldn't usually say because babies, in general, tend to cry a lot. So there's usually no need to point out that this specific baby cries—it's already expected.

- 고양이는 생선을 먹어요.
  Cats eat fish. (a general, universal fact about cats)
- 고양이가 생선을 먹어요.
  The cat eats fish.
  (a specific cat in a particular time or circumstance)

- 친구는 도와줘요.
  Friends help. (a general, universal fact)
- 친구가 도와줘요.
  A (specific) friend helps.

3. When both 은/는 and 이/가 are used in one sentence

Some sentences include both particles.

For example, let's compare the two sentences below.

저는 머리가 길어요. vs. 제 머리는 길어요.

> **VOCAB**
> 머리 hair 길어요 is long

Both sentences mean "I have long hair." Both can be used interchangeably without any grammatical issues, and native speakers will understand you just fine. But if we look at the subtle differences, it mainly comes down to where the focus is.

In **저는 머리가 길어요**, the focus is on **저**(I). This sentence feels more natural in contexts where you're introducing yourself or sharing information about yourself. On the other hand, **제 머리는 길어요** puts the focus not necessarily on **저**(I) but more on **제 머리**(my hair) itself. This sentence would be more appropriate in conversations specifically about your hair.

The next two sentences also work similarly.

제 친구는 성격이 좋아요. vs. 제 친구의 성격은 좋아요.

VOCAB

성격 personality   좋아요 is good

Both sentences mean "My friend has a good personality." On the surface, both sentences are saying the same thing, and you can use them interchangeably without any issues—native speakers will understand you just fine. However, as with the previous examples, the subtle difference lies in where the focus is.

In the first sentence, **제 친구는 성격이 좋아요**, the focus is on **제 친구** (my friend). This makes the sentence more appropriate for situations where you're introducing your friend or providing information about them. On the other hand, in the second sentence, **제 친구의 성격은 좋아요**, the focus is on your friend's personality itself. This sentence is likely to be used most often as a response when someone directly asks you about your friend's personality or when you're specifically discussing personality traits.

I have long hair.

저는 머리가 길어요.
The focus is on 저(I)

제 머리는 길어요.
The focus is on 제 머리(my hair)

My friend has a good personality.

제 친구는 성격이 좋아요.
The focus is on 제 친구(my friend)

제 친구의 성격은 좋아요.
The focus is on 제 친구의 성격
(my friend's personality)

4. 은/는 for Contrast

When you are comparing two or more nouns, especially when those nouns have different characteristics, you can use 은/는 to express contrast.

> *e.g.* 이 책은 재미있어요. 저 책은 재미없어요.
>
> This book is fun. That book is boring.
>
> 선생님은 한국 사람이고 저는 미국 사람이에요.
>
> The teacher is Korean and I'm American.
>
> 저는 바나나는 좋아해요. 근데 레몬은 안 좋아해요.
>
> I like bananas. But I don't like lemons.

5. 이/가 : "It is Noun that~"

이/가 can also be used to emphasize a noun for clarification.

Let's look at some example dialogues first.

> A 누가 우유를 쏟았어요? Who spilled the milk?
> B 제가 그랬어요. I did that.

In **제가 그랬어요**, the particle **이/가** emphasizes that I (and not someone else) spilled the milk. It's like saying, "It is I who did that."

> A 어떤 언어가 제일 재미있어요? Which language is the most fun?
> B 한국어가 제일 재미있어요. Korean is the most fun.

In **한국어가 제일 재미있어요**, the particle **이/가** emphasizes that Korean (and not any other language) is the most fun. It's like saying "It is Korean that is the most fun."

 꿀팁!

Both 은/는 and 이/가 can add emphasis, which can be quite confusing. But it's easier to understand if you recognize that their emphasis works in different ways: 은/는 highlights the main topic of the sentence, providing a broader context, while 이/가 emphasizes a specific noun to clarify details.

To summarize the key differences between the two particles, 은/는 is for ① broad concepts or ② the central topic of a sentence, whereas 이/가 is for ① specific details or ② minor points.

Heads up

As you work through the exercises in this book, you might find yourself wondering whether to use 은/는 or 이/가 when marking the subject in writing practice. Since the example sentences are often short and lack context, it might not always be clear which one to use.

But don't worry! If the choice between 은/는 and 이/가 isn't obvious from the context, I'll specify which one to use in the instructions. So you can focus on practicing without any confusion.

1 Match the following particles with the correct term.

① 이 •

② 은 •

③ 가 •

④ 는 •

• Topic Marker

• Subject Marker

2 저는 and 전 mean the same thing and are interchangeable.

☐ / ☐
TRUE · FALSE

3 When 저 (I) is combined with 가, what is the correct final form?

① 저가   ② 제가   ③ 재가

4 Fill in the blank with the correct topic marker(은/는) for each noun.

① 이름 ☐

② 고양이 ☐

③ 동물 ☐

VOCAB
이름 name
고양이 cat
동물 animal

5 Fill in the blank with the correct subject marker(이/가) for each noun.

① 머리 ☐

② 생선 ☐

③ 성격 ☐

VOCAB
머리 hair, head
생선 fish (for food)
성격 personality

6 Write the correct contraction of each phrase.

① 나 + 는 = [　　　] ② 나 + 가 = [　　　]

③ 너 + 는 = [　　　] ④ 너 + 가 = [　　　]

⑤ 이거 + 가 = [　　　] ⑥ 저 + 의 = [　　　]

7 Topic particles 은/는 can be used to describe a universal characteristic about a noun.

[　] / [　]
TRUE　FALSE

8 In the sentence "친구가 똑똑해요," it refers to a specific friend rather than friends in general.

[　] / [　]
TRUE　FALSE

9 Which particle would you put in the following sentence?

This baby is crying. 아기 [　] 울어요.

10 Which one would sound the most natural in the blank, based on the context?

A 이거 누가 먹었어요? Who ate this?

B (저는 / 제가) 먹었어요. I ate it — It is I who ate it.

ANSWER

1 ①·③ - Subject Marker　②·④ - Topic Marker

2 T　　　　　　　　　　　　　　　**3** ②

4 ① 은 ② 는 ③ 은　　　　　　　　**5** ① 가 ② 이 ③ 이

6 ① 난 ② 내가 ③ 넌 ④ 네가 ⑤ 이게 ⑥ 제

7 T　　　　　　　　**8** T　　　　　　**9** 가

10 제가 (Since the question is asking for clarification about who ate it, it's more natural to use 가 rather than 는.)

Korean Names

If you're interested in Korean actors or K-pop stars, or have lots of Korean friends, you might have already noticed that most Korean names are made up of three syllables. Typically, the surname is one syllable, and the given name is two syllables.

심 효 정

성   이름

(surname)   (given name)

In Korean, the word for surname is **성**, and the word for given name is **이름**. The term **이름** can refer to both the full name (first name and last name combined) and the given name alone.

For example, my Korean name is **심효정**. **심** is the surname, and **효정** is the given name. As you can see, in Korean names, the surname comes first, followed by the given name, which is different from English or other Western names. This reflects a cultural emphasis on family and the idea that the community or family is prioritized over the individual.

While most people have three-syllable names, some have two-syllable names. These names consist of a one-syllable surname and a one-syllable given name. (Such names are called **외자** in Korean.) For instance, in the name **허준**, **허** is the surname, and **준** is the given name, and you can see that their given name consist of just one syllable.

There are also some people that have two-syllable surnames. While most Korean surnames are one syllable, there are a few two-syllable surnames, such as **남궁**, **선우**, and **황보**.
A well-known Korean actor, Namgung Min (**남궁민**), has a two-syllable surname, **남궁**, and a one-syllable given name, **민**. Although these names are rare, they do exist.

In Korean, there is a unique way of addressing or referring to someone by their first name.

❶ First, let's look at how to address someone directly. Depending on the name, you add either **야** or **아** to the end of the name. If the name ends in a vowel, like **민지**(Minji) or **지호**(Jiho), you add **야**.

e.g.

민지야, 놀자! Minji, let's hang out!
지호야, 뭐 해? Jiho, what's up?

On the other hand, if the name ends in a consonant, you add **아**.

효정아, 놀자! Hyojeong, let's hang out!
유진아, 뭐 해? Yujin, what's up?

❷ When referring to someone in conversation with others (not directly calling them), it's different. If the name ends in a vowel, you can simply use the name as is, without having to add another character.

e.g.

어제 민지를 봤어. I saw Minji yesterday.
지호가 날 좋아해. Jiho likes me.

However, if the name ends in a consonant, you must add **이** to the name.

효정이는 착해. Hyojeong is good-hearted.
지호가 유진이를 좋아해. Jiho likes Yujin.

❸ When referring to or addressing someone you're not very close with, it would be considered rude to use just their first name. To maintain politeness, you can add either **씨** or **님** after the name to show respect.

e.g.

유진 씨가 저를 좋아하는 것 같아요. I think Yujin likes me.
민우 님은 어디에서 일하세요? Where do you work, Minu?

CHAPTER 3

을/를
Object Markers

In this chapter, we will learn all the essential basics about the object markers.

1 Objects in a Sentence

1. Word Order

As with 은/는 and 이/가, you mark the object with one of the two object markers 을/를 depending on what the noun ends with.

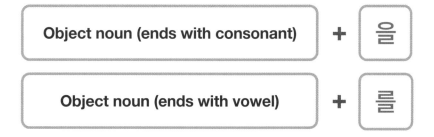

On page 16, we learned about what an "object" is. Now, let's practice identifying the object in each example sentence below.

Sentence	Topic / Subject (noun)	Object (noun)	Verb (action)
❶ 저는 숙제를 해요. I do homework.	저 I	숙제 homework	해 do
❷ 저희는 저녁을 먹었어요. We ate dinner.	저희 We	저녁 dinner	먹었어 ate
❸ 친구가 저를 좋아해요. My friend likes me.	친구 Friend	저 me	좋아해 like

❶ 숙제(homework) is not the doer of the action 해(do,) but rather the target that is directly affected, and it can also be the answer to the question "What are you doing?" Therefore, 숙제 is considered the **object** of 해.

❷ 저녁(dinner) is not the doer of the action 먹었어(ate), but rather the target that is directly affected, and it can also be the answer to the question "What did you eat?" Therefore, **저녁** is considered the **object** of **먹었어**.

❸ **저** (I) is not the doer of the action **좋아해** (like), but rather the target that is directly affected, and it can also be the answer to the question "Whom does your friend like?" Therefore, **저** can be considered the **object** of **좋아해**.

 연습

▶ TRACK 04

Fill in the blank with the correct particles, then identify and write down the topic/subject and object of each sentence.

Sentence	Topic/Subject	Object
① 저는 한국어 ⬚ 배워요. I learn Korean.		
② 빅키 선생님은 과일 ⬚ 좋아해요. Teacher Vicky likes fruits.		

ANSWER
① 를, 저, 한국어 ② 을, 빅키 선생님, 과일

Q I've seen sentences where an object appears before a subject. Is that still grammatically correct?

A
That's correct. A general rule of thumb in Korean sentences is that objects are placed after the subjects. However, if the object is the first thing you'd like the other person to notice, it's perfectly fine to place the object before the subject.

e.g. A 어제 고양이가 연어를 먹었어요.
　　　　My cat ate salmon yesterday.

　　　B 뭘 먹었다고요? What did you say she eat?

　　　A 연어를 고양이가 먹었어요. Salmon, she ate it.

The two words, the original and contracted, are used interchangeably.

저 + 를 → 저를, 절
(I [polite])

나 + 를 → 나를, 날
(I [casual])

너 + 를 → 너를, 널
(you [casual])

이거 + 를 → 이거를, 이걸
(this)

그거 + 를 → 그거를, 그걸
(that)

저거 + 를 → 저거를, 저걸
(that over there)

Quiz

Fill in the blank with the correct forms.

1 선생님이 [   ] 좋아해요.

The teacher likes me.

2 제가 [   ] 먹었어요.

I ate this.

ANSWER

1 저를 / 절

2 이거를 / 이걸

2 은/는 (Topic Markers) vs. 을/를 (Object Markers)

Do you remember from Chapter 2 that the topic of a sentence is not always necessarily a subject and can be an object? This means that just because something is an object in a sentence doesn't mean you always have to use 을/를. If the object is the topic of a sentence, or if you want to emphasize a particular meaning, you can use 은/는 to mark the object instead.

For example, let's say you're a vegetarian and you don't eat meat, so you might want to say, "I don't eat meat." In Korean, you could say, **저는 고기를 안 먹어요**, and that would be fine. But you could also say, **고기는 제가 안 먹어요**.

Here, even though **고기** (meat) is the object of the verb **먹어** (eat), you're focusing on **고기** itself. This shows that it's okay to use 은/는 instead of 을/를 if you want to emphasize it as a main topic.

As we learned in Chapter 2, 은/는 can also be used to compare two or more nouns with different qualities.

For example, let's say you like bananas but not lemons. In this case, the nouns "bananas" and "lemons" are contrasted by their different qualities—one you like, and the other you don't, right? So you can say,

저는 바나나는 좋아해요. 근데 레몬은 안 좋아해요.
I like bananas. But I don't like lemons.

As you can see, even though 바나나 and 레몬 are objects of the verbs 좋아해 (like) and 안 좋아해 (not like), 은/는 is used instead of 을/를 to emphasize the contrast between the two.

Q Does 을/를 add any other meanings or implications?

A

Unlike 은/는 and 이/가, the object particles 을/를 don't add any subtle meanings beyond simply indicating what the object of the sentence is. So there's no need to worry about the complex details.

 꿀팁!

It's common to omit topic, subject, and object marking particles in spoken Korean, unless it's necessary to clarify the subject or object, or you're aiming to add a specific nuance. So, if you're unsure which one to use, it's perfectly fine to remove it and just say the noun.

That said, understanding the differences between 은/는, 이/가, and 을/를 will help you use Korean naturally and fluently in the long run. So, at the beginner level, I encourage you to use these particles as much as possible and really get a feel for how they work.

1 Fill in the blank with the appropriate particle, choosing between subject markers (이/가) and object markers (을/를).

① 친구[ ] 동물[ ] 좋아해요.

My friend likes animals.

② 아기[ ] 울어요.

The baby is crying.

③ 저희 가족[ ] 매일 김치[ ] 먹어요.

My family eats Kimchi every day.

2 Select one INCORRECT form of contraction and write the corrected form in the blank.

① 저를 → 절

② 너를 → 널

③ 이거를 → 이겔

[ ]

3 The only particle that can be used to mark the object in a sentence is 을/를.

[ ] / [ ]
TRUE   FALSE

4 Topic markers 은/는 can be used to emphasize the contrasting qualities of two or more nouns.

☐ / ☐
TRUE   FALSE

5 Each English sentence below is the version translated into Korean. Complete the sentence by filling the blank with the corresponding nouns and particles.
(For particles, use only 이/가 and 을/를.)

① I ate dinner.

→ ☐ ☐ 먹었어요.
　(subject)　　(object)

② This cat is sleeping.

→ ☐ 자요.
　(subject)

③ We like fruit. So we eat it every day.

→ ☐ ☐ 좋아해요. 그래서 매일 먹어요.
　(subject)　　(object)

ANSWER

1　① 가, 을　② 가　③ 이, 를

2　③ 이걸

3　F (In some cases, 은/는 can also be used.)

4　T

5　① 제가, 저녁을　② 고양이가(or 이 고양이가)　③ 저희가, 과일을

My family? Our family?

Have you noticed in one of the Chapter 3 exercises that the Korean term
for "my family" is expressed as **저희 가족**?
While **저희** can mean "we", it also means "our." So why is it that in Korean,
when referring to one's family, people say **저희 가족** or **우리 가족**,
which literally translates to "our family," instead of using
제 가족 or **내 가족** (literally, "my family")?

Generally, when referring to your family as a whole,
it's more common to refer to them as "our" instead of "my."
This reflects the Korean cultural emphasis on collectivism that has been
present for a long time.
Additionally, when referring to family members who are older than you
or even your own home, it's typical to use **저희** or **우리**.

* 저희: we, our (존댓말)
  우리: we, our (반말)

* 우리 is usually used in casual speech (반말), but it can also be used in
  polite speech (존댓말) when you want to be polite without lowering yourself too much,
  such as when speaking to someone much younger.
  This is similar to how 나 (I) can sometimes be used in polite speech.

For example, "older sister" in Korean is 언니 (used by females)
or 누나 (used by males), and when Koreans refer to their own sister,
they typically say 저희/우리 언니 or 저희/우리 누나.
Similarly, "my home" is expressed as 저희 집 or 우리 집,
instead of 제 집 or 내 집.

But, when referring to a friend (친구),
school (학교), or a younger sibling (동생),
it's more common to use 제/내 (my), as in 제 친구, 제 학교,
or 제 동생. That said, you can still use 저희/우리 to refer
to anything, even if it's not your family or home,
if you'd like to add a sense of inclusiveness and intimacy.

CHAPTER 4

Verbs

In this chapter, you'll explore everything you need to know about Korean verbs, including how to conjugate them in the present, past, and future tense.

If someone asked me what the most important part of Korean grammar is, I would without a doubt say, "Verbs!" That's because verbs are usually the key element in a sentence and are rarely left out, aside from very short responses like 네 (yes) or 아니요 (no.)

For example, in Korean, if something is clear from the context, you can often omit it. This is especially true for the subject and object. A classic example is how "I love you" is expressed in Korean.

In the context of telling someone that you love them, it's usually obvious that "I" is the subject and "you" is the object. So "I love you" is simply expressed as 사랑해(요), using only the verb 사랑하다 (to love.)

Since verbs often carry the most weight in a sentence, it's important to know how to use them correctly.

Let's start with a summary of the key points about Korean verbs from Chapter 1.

❶ Verbs are placed at the end of a sentence.

❷ When you use a verb in a sentence, you cannot use the base form as it is and it must be conjugated into the present, past, or future tense according to the respective conjugation rules.

❸ All verbs have a base form that consists of the "stem + 다" structure. For example, in the base form of the verb 살다 (to live), 살 is considered the stem. When a verb is conjugated, the 다 part of the base form should be removed.

In Korean, there is no subject-verb agreement rule like in English. For example, in the English present tense, the verb's form changes depending on whether the subject is singular or plural.

For example,

I am a student. / I study Korean.

She is a student. / She studies Korean.

They are students. / They study Korean.

But there is no such rule in Korean. Whether the subject is singular or plural, you use the same form of verb.

1 Present Tense

First, we will learn how to conjugate verbs in the present tense. Once you understand the present tense conjugation rules, conjugating verbs into the past tense becomes easier because you can simply add specific letters to the present tense form.

1. Various Uses of Present Tense Verbs

❶ It's used to express an action or event currently taking place.

> e.g. 저는 공부해요. I study.

❷ It's used to indicate what is generally the case or someone's or something's usual tendency.

> e.g. 고양이는 생선을 먹어요. Cats eat fish.

❸ It's also used in imperative sentences, including commands, suggestions, and even "let's" statements.

> e.g. 문 닫아. Close the door.
>
> 같이 가요. Let's go together.

❹ It can sometimes express what one plans to do in the future.

> e.g. 저 다음 주에 이사해요. I'm moving next week.

2. Conjugation Rules

The conjugation rules vary depending on the form of a verb stem. While these rules are considered grammatical, they are ultimately designed for the ease of pronunciation for native speakers. By approaching these rules from the perspective of making the language sound smoother, you'll find them easier to understand.

Most conjugation rules depend on the form of the last letter of a verb stem. So, let's first identify the form of the last letter of each stem and then learn the appropriate rules for it.

(1) When a stem ends with a final consonant

Rule 1. Stem + 아

If the last letter of the verb stem ends with a final consonant and they have either ㅏ or ㅗ in the vowel, they're conjugated by adding 아 after the stem.

C : Consonant
F.C : Final Consonant

Base Form	Conjugated (Present Tense)

알다 (to know) ⟶ 알아

살다 (to live) ⟶ 살아

받다 (to receive) ⟶ 받아

닫다 (to close) ⟶ 닫아

앉다 (to sit) ⟶ 앉아

녹다 (to melt) ⟶ 녹아

놀다 (to play, to hang out) ⟶ 놀아

녹다

Quiz

▶ TRACK 06

Fill in the blank with the correct conjugated-form of each verb.

1 빅키 선생님을 [   ] 요. I <u>know</u> teacher Vicky.

2 친구는 한국에 [   ] 요. My friend <u>lives</u> in Korea.

3 문을 [   ] 요. <u>Close</u> the door.

4 친구들하고 [   ] 요. I <u>hang out</u> with my friends.

* In Korean, the subject and object are often omitted when they are obvious from the context. This is especially common when "I" is the subject. In this book, you will frequently see sentences where 저는 or 제가 is omitted.

ANSWER

1 알아 2 살아 3 닫아 4 놀아

63

Rule 2. Stem + 어

If the last letter of the verb stem ends with a final consonant and the vowel is <u>anything other than ㅏ or ㅗ</u>, the verb is conjugated by adding 어 after the stem.

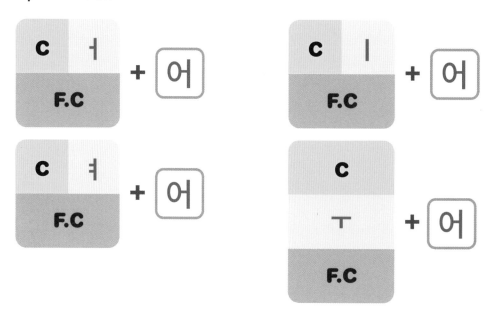

Base Form		Conjugated (Present Tense)
먹다 (to eat)	⟶	먹어
입다 (to wear, to put on)	⟶	입어
읽다 (to read)	⟶	읽어
열다 (to open)	⟶	열어
웃다 (to smile, to laugh)	⟶	웃어
울다 (to cry)	⟶	울어 울다

Due to space constraints, not all vowels could be included on this page, but this rule applies to all vowels except ㅏ and ㅗ. For example, 만들다 (to make) becomes **만들어**.

(Exceptions: ㅑ and ㅛ, as they are phonetically similar to ㅏ and ㅗ. However, since very few verbs end with ㅑ or ㅛ, they don't need to be given much consideration.)

Quiz

▶ **TRACK 07**

Fill in the blank with the correct conjugated-form of each verb.

1 매일 한국 음식을 [   ] 요.

I <u>eat</u> Korean food every day.

2 제 여동생은 매일 바지를 [   ] 요.

My younger sister <u>wears</u> pants every day.

3 책을 많이 [   ] 요.

I <u>read</u> a lot of books.

4 문 [   ] . [in 반말, the casual speech]

<u>Open</u> the door.

5 이 아기는 매일 [   ] 요.

This baby <u>cries</u> every day.

ANSWER

1 먹어 2 입어

3 읽어 4 열어

5 울어

---

(2) When a stem ends only with a vowel

> ### Rule 3. Stem
> **(only the stem itself — nothing added to it)**

❶ If a verb stem ends in ㅏ, you can conjugate the verb using just the stem without needing to add anything.

Here's an additional explanation that might be helpful. I mentioned earlier that when remembering conjugation rules, it helps to think from the perspective of

65

pronunciation ease, right? It's related to that.

If a verb's stem ends in ㅏ or ㅗ, the conjugation rule is to add 아. However, when you add 아 to a stem that already ends in ㅏ (and has no final consonant), the 아 becomes phonetically redundant because the ㅏ sound is already present in the stem.

Adding an extra 아 would only lengthen the ㅏ [a] sound, which is unnecessary from a pronunciation standpoint. Therefore, the rule ends up being that you can just use the stem alone.

Base Form		Conjugated (Present Tense)
가다	(to go) ⟶	**가**
만나다	(to meet) ⟶	**만나**
사다	(to buy) ⟶	**사**
자다	(to sleep) ⟶	**자**

사다

Quiz

▶ TRACK 08

Fill in the blank with the correct conjugated-form of each verb.

1 평일에 학교에 [　　] 요.

 I go to school on weekdays.

2 주말에 친구를 [　　] 요.

 I meet my friend on the weekend.

3 고양이 사료를 많이 [　　] 요.

 I buy a lot of cat food.

4 엄마는 일찍 [　　] 요.

 Mom sleeps early.

ANSWER

1 가   **2** 만나

3 사   **4** 자

❷ **If a verb stem ends in either ㅓ, ㅕ or ㅐ, you can conjugate the verb using just the stem without needing to add anything.**

Similar to the previous example, this can also be understood easily from the perspective of pronunciation ease.

If a verb's stem ends in a vowel other than ㅏ or ㅗ, the conjugation rule is to add 어. However, for verbs ending in ㅓ [eo] or ㅕ [yeo], since both already contain the 어 [eo] sound, adding 어 would be phonetically redundant and would only lengthen the ㅓ sound.

Additionally, for verbs ending in ㅐ, adding 어 and pronouncing them together can feel somewhat awkward. Therefore, it's more natural and easier to simply use the stem alone for conjugation.

Base Form		Conjugated (Present Tense)
서다	(to stand) ⟶	서
켜다	(to turn on) ⟶	켜
보내다	(to send) ⟶	보내

켜다

Quiz

Fill in the blank with the correct conjugated-form of each verb.

1 불 [____]. [in 반말, the casual speech]

Turn on the light.

2 여기 [____]. [in 반말, the casual speech]

Stand here.

3 선생님께 편지를 [____]요.

I send an email to the teacher.

ANSWER
1 켜 2 서 3 보내

Rules 4 through 6 involve changing the vowel in the verb stem to a different one. This replacement isn't random and it rather reflects phonetically natural patterns.

Rule 4. Replace ㅗ with ㅘ

If a verb stem ends in ㅗ, you can conjugate it by replacing that ㅗ with the vowel ㅘ.

c ㅗ + 아 → c ㅘ

This rule also reflects the phonetic ease that I mentioned earlier.

We know that verbs ending in ㅏ or ㅗ are conjugated by adding **아**, and when you add **아** to a verb stem that ends in ㅗ, the combination of ㅗ and **아** produces the diphthong sound ㅘ [wa] when spoken quickly. Therefore, the rule simplifies this by directly combining ㅗ and **아** into ㅘ.

Base Form	Conjugated (Present Tense)

오다 (to come) ⟶ 와

보다 (to see, to watch) ⟶ 봐

보다

Quiz

▶ TRACK 10

Fill in the blank with the correct conjugated-form of each verb.

1   비가 ☐ 요.

It's raining. (Literally, the rain comes.)

2   한국 드라마를 ☐ 요.

I watch Korean dramas.

ANSWER

1 와   **2** 봐

Rule 5. Replace ㅜ with ㅝ

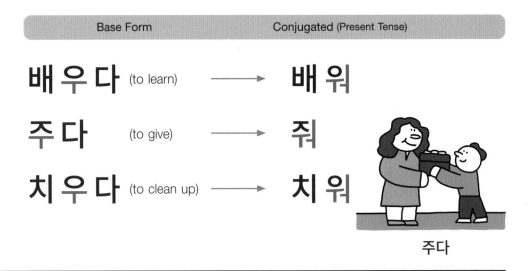

This rule also reflects phonetic ease.

We know that verbs ending in a vowel that is anything other than ㅏ or ㅗ are conjugated by adding 어, and when you add 어 to a verb stem that ends in ㅜ, the combination of ㅜ and 어 produces the diphthong sound ㅝ [wo] when spoken quickly. Therefore, the rule simplifies this by directly combining ㅜ and 어 into ㅝ.

Base Form	Conjugated (Present Tense)
배우다 (to learn) →	배워
주다 (to give) →	줘
치우다 (to clean up) →	치워

주다

Quiz

▶ TRACK 11

Fill in the blank with the correct conjugated-form of each verb.

1 저는 한국어를 [   ]요.

   I <u>learn</u> Korean.

2 매일 방을 [   ]요.

   I <u>clean up</u> my room every day.

ANSWER

1 배워 2 치워

Rule 6. Replace ㅣ with ㅕ

ㄷㅣ + 어 → ㄷㅕ

For verbs ending in the ㅣ vowel, you also add 어 when conjugating, but when ㅣ and 어 are pronounced quickly together, they form the diphthong sound ㅕ [yeo]. The rule simplifies this by directly combining ㅣ and 어 into ㅕ.

Base Form	Conjugated (Present Tense)
마시다 (to drink) ⟶	마셔
가르치다 (to teach) ⟶	가르쳐

마시다

Quiz

▶ TRACK 12

Fill in the blank with the correct conjugated-form of each verb.

1 아침에 커피를 [＿＿＿＿]요.

I **drink** coffee in the morning.

2 빅키 선생님은 한국어를 [＿＿＿＿]요.

Teacher Vicky **teaches** Korean.

ANSWER
1 마셔 2 가르쳐

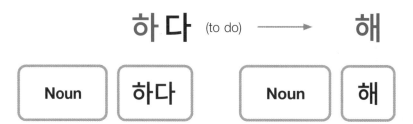

Rule 7. All −하다 verbs are conjugated to 해

하다 (to do) ⟶ **해**

| Noun | 하다 | | Noun | 해 |

하다 itself is a Korean verb that means "to do." There are many Korean verbs that include **하다**, and in these cases, a noun is usually combined with the verb **하다** to form a fixed verb.

For example, the verb **공부하다** (to study) is formed by combining the noun **공부** (studying) with the verb **하다** (to do), resulting in the meaning "to study."

Similarly, the verb **운전하다** (to drive) is created by combining the noun **운전** (driving) with the verb **하다**, forming the verb "to drive."

However, there are also some verbs that contain **하다** but don't go with a noun. For instance, in the verb **좋아하다** (to like), **좋아** is not a noun. Nevertheless, since the verb ends with **하다**, it follows the same conjugation rules as other verbs ending in **하다**.

| Base Form | Conjugated (Present Tense) |

공부하다 (to study) ⟶ **공부해**

운전하다 (to drive) ⟶ **운전해**

운동하다 (to exercise, to work out) ⟶ **운동해**

일하다 (to work) ⟶ **일해**

좋아하다 (to like) ⟶ **좋아해**

좋아하다

Quiz

Fill in the blank with the correct conjugated-form of each verb.

1 도서관에서 [   ] 요.

I <u>study</u> at a library.

2 헬스장에서 [   ] 요.

I <u>work out</u> at a gym.

3 한국 사람들을 [   ] 요.

I <u>like</u> Korean people.

ANSWER

1 공부해   2 운동해   3 좋아해

3. Irregular Conjugation Rules

All the rules we've learned so far fall under regular rules. A lot of Korean verbs fall into this category, and with these rules in mind, you can conjugate the majority of verbs correctly.

However, there are exceptions with irregular verbs. As the name suggests, irregular verbs are those that follow different rules from the regular ones we've learned so far.

For now, let's focus on the three most common irregular verbs. Irregular verbs can be a bit tricky since they follow different patterns, so we won't dive into specific rules yet. Instead, I suggest simply memorizing the final forms of these verbs for now.

Base Form	Conjugated (Present Tense)

듣다 (to listen, to hear) ⟶ 들어

쓰다 (to write, to use) ⟶ 써

모르다 (to not know) ⟶ 몰라

쓰다

Quiz

▶ TRACK 14

Fill in the blank with the correct conjugated-form of each verb.

1 무슨 음악을 [   ]요?

What music do you <u>listen to</u>?

2 선생님은 한국어 교재를 [   ]요.

The teacher <u>writes</u> Korean textbooks.

3 [   ]요.

I <u>don't know</u>.

ANSWER
1 들어 2 써 3 몰라

Past Tense

Once you understand how the present tense is conjugated, the past tense becomes very simple and straightforward. It always follows a consistent rule: simply add the final consonant ㅆ and 어 to the present tense conjugated form.

Past Tense Conjugation

Present Tense + ㅆ + 어

As you may have noticed, all present tense conjugated forms end with a vowel. So, you just add the ㅆ final consonant to that vowel and then attach 어 as the next syllable.

To demonstrate, let's take some of the verbs we learned earlier in the present tense section.

	Present Tense	**Past Tense**
살다	살아	살았어 [사라써]
먹다	먹어	먹었어 [머거써]
웃다	웃어	웃었어 [우서써]
가다	가	갔어 [가써]
오다	와	왔어 [와써]
하다	해	했어 [해써]
모르다	몰라	몰랐어 [몰라써]

* The words in brackets represent how they're pronounced.

It's also easy to remember when speaking, because when ㅆ and 어 are combined, they are pronounced as 써 , blending together due to the **consonant assimilation rule**. So, when you want to use a verb in the past tense, you just add 써 to the present tense form.

 연습

Now, let's practice conjugating the rest of the verbs we learned.

This will give you a chance to work on both present and past tense conjugations.

Start by filling in the table on your own, and then check your answers.

	Present Tense	Past Tense
알다 (to know)		
받다 (to receive)		
닫다 (to close)		
앉다 (to sit)		
녹다 (to melt)		
놀다 (to play, to hang out)		
입다 (to wear, to put on)		
읽다 (to read)		
열다 (to open)		
웃다 (to smile, to laugh)		
울다 (to cry)		
만들다 (to make)		
만나다 (to meet)		
사다 (to buy)		
자다 (to sleep)		

	Present Tense	Past Tense
서다 (to stand)		
켜다 (to turn on)		
보내다 (to send)		
보다 (to see, to watch)		
배우다 (to learn)		
주다 (to give)		
치우다 (to clean up)		
마시다 (to drink)		
가르치다 (to teach)		
공부하다 (to study)		
운전하다 (to drive)		
운동하다 (to work out)		
일하다 (to work)		
좋아하다 (to like)		
듣다 (to listen, to hear)		
쓰다 (to write, to use)		

ANSWER

	Present Tense	Past Tense
알다 (to know)	알아	알았어
받다 (to receive)	받아	받았어
닫다 (to close)	닫아	닫았어
앉다 (to sit)	앉아	앉았어
녹다 (to melt)	녹아	녹았어
놀다 (to play, to hang out)	놀아	놀았어
입다 (to wear, to put on)	입어	입었어
읽다 (to read)	읽어	읽었어
열다 (to open)	열어	열었어
웃다 (to smile, to laugh)	웃어	웃었어
울다 (to cry)	울어	울었어
만들다 (to make)	만들어	만들었어
만나다 (to meet)	만나	만났어
사다 (to buy)	사	샀어
자다 (to sleep)	자	잤어
서다 (to stand)	서	섰어
켜다 (to turn on)	켜	켰어
보내다 (to send)	보내	보냈어

	Present Tense	Past Tense
보다 (to see, to watch)	봐	봤어
배우다 (to learn)	배워	배웠어
주다 (to give)	줘	줬어
치우다 (to clean up)	치워	치웠어
마시다 (to drink)	마셔	마셨어
가르치다 (to teach)	가르쳐	가르쳤어
공부하다 (to study)	공부해	공부했어
운전하다 (to drive)	운전해	운전했어
운동하다 (to work out)	운동해	운동했어
일하다 (to work)	일해	일했어
좋아하다 (to like)	좋아해	좋아했어
듣다 (to listen, to hear)	들어	들었어
쓰다 (to write, to use)	써	썼어

3 Future Tense

1. Regular Conjugation Rules

While the conjugation rules for present and past tenses are related, the future tense follows a completely different set of rules.

First, the future tense has different forms for polite (**존댓말**) and casual (**반말**) speech. In the present and past tense, you just conjugate the verb and then add **요** to make it a polite speech, right? It works similarly for the future tense, but in a slightly different way.

Let's start with the pattern that applies to both forms of speech when conjugating a verb in the future tense :

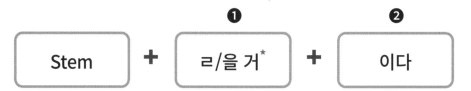

* Both 거 and 것 are correct, but in everyday speech, 거 is used more commonly.

To demonstrate, let's conjugate the verbs **먹다** (to eat) and **마시다** (to drink) into the future tense.

❶ First, add either the consonant ㄹ or the syllable 을 to the verb stem. You may have already noticed this pattern as you've been learning Korean grammar: the choice depends on whether the verb stem ends in a vowel or a consonant.

If the verb stem ends in a vowel, you add ㄹ; if it ends in a consonant, you add 을. After that, you attach 거.

먹 + 을 거 = 먹을 거

마시 + ㄹ 거 = 마실 거

 꿀팁!

The −ㄹ/을 suffix sounds like the "l" sound in English, similar to "will," making it easy to remember as a suffix for the future tense.

❷ Next, you need to conjugate the verb 이다. You may have learned about 이다 in detail in my previous book, *All-You-Need Korean for Absolute Beginners*. But if you haven't started with that book or aren't familiar with how 이다 works, don't worry! We'll cover it more thoroughly in the next chapter.

For now, it's enough to note that 이다 is a bit of a unique "verb" because the conjugation changes depending on whether the preceding noun ends in a vowel or a consonant. Since the word 거 (which is actually a noun that means "thing") ends in a vowel, you attach 예요 to it. In casual speech, the form changes, and you attach 야 instead.

So when conjugating into the future tense, it looks like this:

• **will eat**

먹을 거예요 - polite (존댓말)

먹을 거야 - casual (반말)

e.g. 저녁으로 김치찌개를 먹을 거예요.
I will eat Kimchi Stew for dinner.

• **will drink**

마실 거예요 - polite (존댓말)

마실 거야 - casual (반말)

e.g. 물을 마실 거예요.
I will drink water.

So, you can remember the future tense conjugation rule as follows:

> **Polite future tense: Stem + 르/을 + 거예요**

> **Casual future tense: Stem + 르/을 + 거야**

This is the most general (and regular) way to express Korean verbs in the future tense.

2. Irregular Conjugation Rules

Of course, there are also irregular verbs in the future tense. For now, let's focus on the most common ones.

Interestingly, some verbs become irregular only when conjugated into the future tense. On the other hand, some verbs are the exact opposite—they are irregular in the present and past tenses but follow the regular future tense conjugation rule.

(1) ㄹ-ending Verbs

For example, all verbs ending in ㄹ follow the regular conjugation rules in the present and past tenses (e.g., **살아, 살았어**). However, when conjugating them into the future tense, they follow the irregular rule.

살다 → 살을 거예요 (X)
　　　살 거예요　　(O) (will live)

알다 → 알을 거예요 (X)
　　　알 거예요　　(O) (will know)

As you can see, there's no need to attach the extra **을** suffix to the stem. You simply use the stem as it is and add **거예요** or **거야**.

> **ㄹ-ending Verbs' Future Tense: Stem + 거예요/거야**

(2) Irregular in Present & Past Tense, Regular in Future Tense

In contrast, there are some irregular verbs that follow the regular rule only when conjugated into the future tense. For instance, we've learned that 모르다 is irregular in the present and past tense (몰라, 몰랐어). However, in the future tense, it follows the regular rule:

모르 + ㄹ + 거예요 = 모를 거예요 (will not know)

The same applies to 쓰다, which conjugates to 쓸 거예요 (will write) in the future tense.

(3) Irregular in All Tenses

Lastly, there are verbs that are irregular in all tenses — present, past, and future. 듣다 (to listen) is the most common and notable example.

듣다's future conjugation : 들을 거예요. (The final consonant ㄷ changes to ㄹ, and then the extra 을 suffix is added.)

The future tense is used not only for personal plans but also for making predictions about the future.

> *e.g.* 내일 비가 올 거예요. It will rain tomorrow.
>
> 날씨가 따뜻할 거예요. (따뜻하다: to be warm — adjective)
> The weather will be warm.

You can also use adverbs like 아마 (maybe, perhaps, probably) to express a less certain likelihood.

> *e.g.* 아마 비가 올 거예요. It will probably rain.
>
> 아마 따뜻할 거예요. It will probably be warm.

There are actually a few other ways to express the future tense in Korean, such as −겠어요, −ㄹ/을게요, and so on, each with its own usage and nuance. Since −ㄹ/을 거 + 이다 is the most common and basic way to express the future tense, this book will focus on helping you master this particular grammar pattern first.

연습

Now that you've learned how to conjugate verbs in the future tense, let's fill in the table below. Be sure to distinguish between polite (**존댓말**) and casual (**반말**) forms.

	Future Tense in 존댓말	Future Tense in 반말
살다 (to live)		
알다 (to know)		
받다 (to receive)		
닫다 (to close)		
앉다 (to sit)		
녹다 (to melt)		
놀다 (to play, to hang out)		
먹다 (to eat)		
입다 (to wear, to put on)		
읽다 (to read)		
열다 (to open)		
웃다 (to smile, to laugh)		
울다 (to cry)		
만들다 (to make)		
만나다 (to meet)		
사다 (to buy)		

	Future Tense in 존댓말	Future Tense in 반말
자다 (to sleep)		
서다 (to stand)		
켜다 (to turn on)		
보내다 (to send)		
보다 (to see, to watch)		
배우다 (to learn)		
주다 (to give)		
치우다 (to clean up)		
마시다 (to drink)		
가르치다 (to teach)		
공부하다 (to study)		
운전하다 (to drive)		
운동하다 (to work out)		
일하다 (to work)		
좋아하다 (to like)		
듣다 (to listen, to hear)		
쓰다 (to write, to use)		
모르다 (to not know)		

ANSWER

	Future Tense in 존댓말	Future Tense in 반말
살다 (to live)	살 거예요	살 거야
알다 (to know)	알 거예요	알 거야
받다 (to receive)	받을 거예요	받을 거야
닫다 (to close)	닫을 거예요	닫을 거야
앉다 (to sit)	앉을 거예요	앉을 거야
녹다 (to melt)	녹을 거예요	녹을 거야
놀다 (to play, to hang out)	놀 거예요	놀 거야
먹다 (to eat)	먹을 거예요	먹을 거야
입다 (to wear, to put on)	입을 거예요	입을 거야
읽다 (to read)	읽을 거예요	읽을 거야
열다 (to open)	열 거예요	열 거야
웃다 (to smile, to laugh)	웃을 거예요	웃을 거야
울다 (to cry)	울 거예요	울 거야
만들다 (to make)	만들 거예요	만들 거야
만나다 (to meet)	만날 거예요	만날 거야
사다 (to buy)	살 거예요	살 거야
자다 (to sleep)	잘 거예요	잘 거야
서다 (to stand)	설 거예요	설 거야

	Future Tense in 존댓말	Future Tense in 반말
켜다 (to turn on)	켤 거예요	켤 거야
보내다 (to send)	보낼 거예요	보낼 거야
보다 (to see, to watch)	볼 거예요	볼 거야
배우다 (to learn)	배울 거예요	배울 거야
주다 (to give)	줄 거예요	줄 거야
치우다 (to clean up)	치울 거예요	치울 거야
마시다 (to drink)	마실 거예요	마실 거야
가르치다 (to teach)	가르칠 거예요	가르칠 거야
공부하다 (to study)	공부할 거예요	공부할 거야
운전하다 (to drive)	운전할 거예요	운전할 거야
운동하다 (to work out)	운동할 거예요	운동할 거야
일하다 (to work)	일할 거예요	일할 거야
좋아하다 (to like)	좋아할 거예요	좋아할 거야
듣다 (to listen, to hear)	들을 거예요	들을 거야
쓰다 (to write, to use)	쓸 거예요	쓸 거야
모르다 (to not know)	모를 거예요	모를 거야

1 Write the <u>present tense</u> conjugation of each verb and match it to its correct meaning.

① 알다 [   ] •   • to teach

② 모르다 [   ] •   • to learn

③ 웃다 [   ] •   • to know

④ 배우다 [   ] •   • to laugh

⑤ 가르치다 [   ] •   • to not know

⑥ 사다 [   ] •   • to see

⑦ 보다 [   ] •   • to buy

⑧ 보내다 [   ] •   • to send

2 Find the INCORRECTLY conjugated verb and rewrite it correctly.

① 저는 매일 <u>운동해요</u>. I work out every day.

② 이메일을 <u>보내요</u>. I send an email.

③ 커피를 좀 <u>마셔요</u>. Drink some coffee.

④ 우리 집으로 <u>오요</u>. Come to my house.

⑤ 저는 평일에 학교에 <u>가요</u>. I go to school on weekdays.

[   ]

3 Circle all the verbs below that use <u>only the stem</u> when conjugated in the present tense.

먹다	보다	오다	주다	가다
사다	자다	마시다	켜다	보내다
서다	만나다	쓰다		

4 Conjugate the following verbs in each tense using the –요 ending 존댓말.

	Present Tense	Past Tense	Future Tense
① 앉다 (to sit)			
② 울다 (to cry)			
③ 만나다 (to meet)			
④ 서다 (to stand)			
⑤ 일하다 (to work)			
⑥ 듣다 (to listen)			

5 Choose the INCORRECTLY conjugated verb in the future tense and write the correct form.

① 살 거예요 will live   ② 알 거예요 will know

③ 몰 거예요 will not know   ④ 닫을 거예요 will close

⑤ 열 거예요 will open

6 Fill in the blank with the correct verb conjugated in the given tense.

① 제 남동생은 책을 많이 [   ]요.

My younger brother reads a lot of books.

② 편지를 [   ]요.

I received a letter.

③ 오늘 청바지를 [   ]요.

I will wear jeans today.

④ 친구를 [   ]요.

I met a friend.

⑤ 라디오를 [   ]요.

I turned on the radio.

7 Write the following sentences in the −요 ending 존댓말. For sentences where "I" is the subject, omit "I" when writing. Use the particles 이/가 and 을/를.

① The teacher knows my name.

_____

② My friend studies Korean. (Korean [language]: 한국어)

_____

③ I closed the door.

_____

④ Open the window. (window: 창문)

_____

⑤ I will learn Korean.

_____

ANSWER

1 ① 알아 (to know) ② 몰라 (to not know) ③ 웃어 (to laugh) ④ 배워 (to learn) ⑤ 가르쳐 (to teach)
   ⑥ 사 (to buy) ⑦ 봐 (to see) ⑧ 보내 (to send)

2 ④ 와

3 가다, 사다, 자다, 켜다, 보내다, 서다, 만나다

4 ① 앉아요, 앉았어요, 앉을 거예요 ② 울어요, 울었어요, 울 거예요 ③ 만나요, 만났어요, 만날 거예요
   ④ 서요, 섰어요, 설 거예요 ⑤ 일해요, 일했어요, 일할 거예요 ⑥ 들어요, 들었어요, 들을 거예요

5 ③ 모를 거예요

6 ① 읽어 ② 받았어 ③ 입을 거에 ④ 만났어 ⑤ 켰어

7 ① 선생님이 제 이름을 알아요. ② (제) 친구가 한국어를 공부해요. ③ 문을 닫았어요. ④ 창문을 열어요.
   ⑤ 한국어를 배울 거예요.

What to Wear in Korean?

In this chapter, we learned **입다** is the verb that means "to wear."

But did you know that in Korean, different verbs are used for wearing, depending on which body part you're putting something on?

Generally, **입다** is used for all clothing worn on the upper and lower body, from the shoulders to the legs.

> e.g. 티셔츠를 입어요.
> 코트를 입어요.
> 바지를 입어요.

쓰다 is used for items worn on the head or face.

> e.g. 모자를 써요.
> 안경을 써요.
> 마스크를 써요.

신다 is used for items worn on the feet.

> e.g. 양말을 신어요.
> 신발을 신어요.

Also, for things worn around the neck (like scarf or muffler), we use the verb **매다**, and for things worn on the hands (like gloves or rings), we use **끼다**.

> e.g. 목도리를 매요. I put on a muffler.
> 장갑을 껴요. I put on gloves.

CHAPTER 5

Essential Opposite
Verb Pairs in Korean

This chapter covers 5 essential verb pairs with opposite
meanings. The reason these verbs are covered in a separate
chapter is that they are not only very common, but they can
also be quite counterintuitive to non-native learners. This
chapter will help you learn these pairs more effectively and
ensure they are easier to remember.

1   to be or not to be

First, we will learn about the verbs **이다** and **아니다**.

Technically speaking, **이다** is classified as a particle and **아니다** as an adjective. However, since **이다** functions as a "descriptive" particle, it is often referred to as a "verb" for convenience. Similarly, while **아니다** is technically an adjective, another term for adjectives is a descriptive "verb," so it, too, is commonly considered a verb.

1. 이다: to be

이다 translates to "to be," but it's not exactly the same as the English "to be." The key difference is that **이다** can only be used with nouns.
This means it can only express "to be" in the context of "to be + noun"
(for example, "I am a student," "It is a bird," "They are my friends" etc.).
It cannot be used with adjectives that describe a state or quality
(for example, "I am smart," "My brother is tall," etc.).

Since **이다** functions like a verb, it can be conjugated into present, past, and future tense. However, unlike other verbs,
the conjugation changes depending on whether the noun it's paired with ends in a vowel or a consonant. This results in two different conjugation forms depending on the noun.

First, let's take a look at some example sentences using **이다**.

그 사람은 의사예요.
That person is a doctor.

저는 학생이에요.
I am a student.

As you can see, since **이다** functions like a verb, it appears at the end of a sentence.

A key difference in word order between English and Korean is that in English, you say "to be + noun," while in Korean, it follows the order of "noun + 이다."

When the preceding noun ends in a vowel (e.g., 의사 [ㅏ]), it conjugates to 예요. If the noun ends in a consonant (e.g., 학생 [ㅇ]), it conjugates to 이에요.

Another important point to note is that, as mentioned earlier, 이다 is officially referred to as a "descriptive particle." Since it's essentially a particle, it must follow a noun directly without any space, just like other particles in Korean. Therefore, instead of writing 의사 예요 or 학생 이에요 with a space, the correct form is 의사예요 and 학생이에요 without any space in between.

The verb 이다 is unique compared to other verbs in that its conjugation differs between formal and informal speech. Do you remember when we covered future tense conjugation in Chapter 4? We learned that because future tense also ends with 이다, the formal and informal forms conjugate differently, right?

The 존댓말(polite) and 반말(casual) forms of 이다 are as follows:

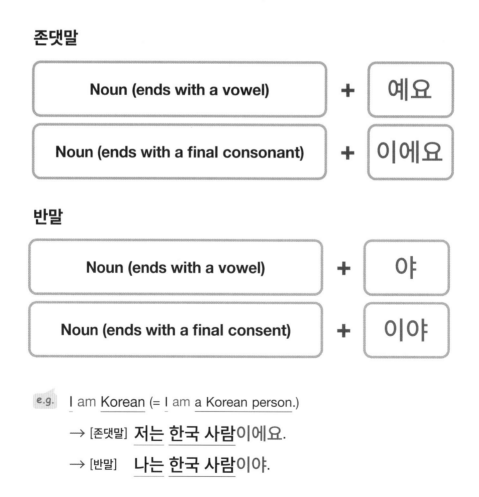

존댓말

Noun (ends with a vowel)	+ 예요
Noun (ends with a final consonant)	+ 이에요

반말

Noun (ends with a vowel)	+ 야
Noun (ends with a final consent)	+ 이야

e.g. I am Korean (= I am a Korean person.)

→ [존댓말] 저는 한국 사람이에요.

→ [반말] 나는 한국 사람이야.

My friend is a chef.

→ [존댓말] 제 친구는 요리사예요.

→ [반말] 내 친구는 요리사야.

 In a Nutshell

이다 is a descriptive particle that functions both as a particle and a verb.

Its conjugation changes depending on whether the preceding noun ends with a vowel or a consonant.

It also has different forms depending on whether you're using 존댓말 (polite speech) or 반말 (informal speech).

It is Noun.	존댓말	반말
Noun (ends with a vowel)	예요	야
Noun (ends with a consonant)	이에요	이야

Quiz

▶ TRACK 17

Fill in the blank with the correct form of 이다 in the –요 ending 존댓말.

1 제 이름 [   ]. It's my name.

2 책 [   ]. It's a book.

3 고양이 [   ]. It's a cat.

4 지수는 제 친구 [   ]. Jisu is my friend.

ANSWER

1 이에요   2 이에요   3 예요   4 예요

95

2. 아니다 : to not be

The antonym of **이다** is **아니다**.

To express that something or someone is "not Noun," you can use the structure **Noun + 이/가 아니다**, where you add the particle **이** or **가** depending on whether the noun ends in a vowel or a consonant. (It is also common to omit **이/가** in usage.)

아니다 also has separate conjugation forms for polite and casual forms. It conjugates to **아니에요** for polite speech and **아니야** for casual speech.

> *e.g.* I am not a student.
>
> → [존댓말] **저는 학생이 아니에요.** (or **학생 아니에요.**)
>
> → [반말] **나는 학생이 아니야.** (or **학생 아니야.**)
>
> It is not a vegetable.
>
> → [존댓말] **채소가 아니에요.** (or **채소 아니에요.**)
>
> → [반말] **채소가 아니야.** (or **채소 아니야.**)
>
> * Unlike 이다, 아니다 is not a particle. Therefore, you need to add the particle 이/가 after the noun, or even if you omit the particle, there should still be a space between the noun and 아니다.

 In a Nutshell

- Noun **이/가 아니다** : It is not Noun. (It's also possible to omit the particle **이/가**.)
- It has different forms depending on whether you're using **존댓말** (polite speech) or **반말** (informal speech).

It is not Noun.	존댓말	반말
Noun (ends with a vowel)	(가) 아니에요	(가) 아니야
Noun (ends with a consonant)	(이) 아니에요	(이) 아니야

1   Select one WRONG way to write "It's not a bird" in Korean.

     ① 새가 아니에요.

     ② 새 아니에요.

     ③ 새아니에요.

2   Fill in the blank with the correct words in the −요 ending 존댓말.

저는 선생님 [＿＿＿＿＿]. 학생 [＿＿＿＿＿].

I'm not a teacher. I'm a student.

3   Write the following sentence in Korean using 이다 and 아니다 in 반말.

It's not a fruit. It's a vegetable.

→ [＿＿＿＿＿＿＿＿＿＿]

ANSWER

1 ③   2 (이) 아니에요, 이에요   3 과일(이) 아니야. 채소야.

Q   **What about the other tenses of 이다 and 아니다?**

A

이다	Present Tense	Past Tense	Future Tense
존댓말	예요(vowel)/ 이에요(consonant)	였어요(vowel)/ 이었어요(consonant)	일 거예요
반말	야/이야	였어/이었어	일 거야

아니다	Present Tense	Past Tense	Future Tense
존댓말	아니에요	아니었어요	아닐 거예요
반말	아니야	아니었어	아닐 거야

2 │ to exist or not exist / to have or not have

The next pair is 있다 and 없다.

These two verbs are antonyms and they have two main meanings. One meaning expresses **existence** as in "There is / There isn't" and the other expresses **possession** as in "to have / to not have."

Let's start by looking at the usage of 있다.

있다

있다 is a regular verb, so it follows the regular rules when being conjugated.

있다	Present Tense	Past Tense	Future Tense
반말	있어	있었어	있을 거야
존댓말	있어요	있었어요	있을 거예요

When learning about 있다, the most important thing to focus on is the particles it follows.

있다 takes the particle 이/가, whether it is used to express existence or possession.

(Depending on the context and the meaning you want to convey, such as contrast or emphasis, it can be replaced with 은/는 as well.)

e.g. ❶ **existence**

나무가 있어요.
There is a tree.

책상이 있어요.
There is a desk.

❷ possession

시계가 있어요.

I have a clock/watch.

동생이 있어요.

I have a younger sibling.

The reason I'm emphasizing 이/가 is that many learners often make the mistake of using 을/를 with 있다. This happens especially because in English, 있다 is translated as "to have something," where "something" becomes the object of "have," leading learners to intuitively use 을/를.

However, the primary meaning of 있다 is actually "to exist" so even when it's used to express possession, it's correct to use 이/가, not 을/를.

Of course, 이/가 can be omitted, and you can simply use "Noun + 있다" either to indicate existence or possession. But at the beginner level, it's recommended to practice using the subject maker without omitting it.

없다

Once you understand the usage of 있다, learning about 없다 is a piece of cake. The two verbs differ only in meaning, and the other usage rules apply in the same way.

없다 is also a regular verb, so it follows the regular rules when being conjugated.

없다	Present Tense	Past Tense	Future Tense
반말	없어	없었어	없을 거야
존댓말	없어요	없었어요	없을 거예요

Same with 있다, 없다 is also used with the 이/가 particle.

(Likewise, if you want to add emphasis or contrast, you can replace it with 은/는. But you cannot use it with 을/를.)

e.g. **❶ existence**

나무가 없어요.

There is no tree.

책상이 없어요.

There is no desk.

❷ possession

시계가 없어요.

I don't have a clock/watch.

동생이 없어요.

I don't have a younger sibling.

이/가 can be omitted, so using just "**Noun + 없다**" is also acceptable.

Quiz

▶ **TRACK 19**

1 Fill in the blank with the correct particle.

① 직업 ⬚ 있어요. I have a job.

② 한국인 친구 ⬚ 없어요. I don't have a Korean friend.

2 Select one meaning that the sentence below does NOT represent.

집이 있어요.

① I have a house.

② There's a house.

③ I'm at a house.

ANSWER

1 ① 이 ② 가

2 ③ (While you can use 있다 to say "I'm at a house," a different particle should be used. The correct expression is 집에 있어요. We will learn more about the particle 에 in Chapter 6.)

3 to become

되다

되다 means "to become." Let's start by looking at its conjugation.

Since 되다 is a regular verb and its stem ends with the vowel ㅚ, the rule is to add 어 when conjugating it into the present tense. So it becomes 되어, but in many cases, it's shortened to 돼.

Both 되어 and 돼 are correct, but in this book, we will primarily use 돼.

되다	Present Tense	Past Tense	Future Tense
반말	돼 (되어)	됐어 (되었어)	될 거야
존댓말	돼요 (되어요)	됐어요 (되었어요)	될 거예요

되다 means "to become something", so it is used together with a noun that represents that "something." From an English perspective, it might seem natural to use 을/를 since "something" appears to be the object of "become."

However, 되다 must be followed by the 이/가 particle, not 을/를. (Unless you want to use 은/는 to indicate contrast.)

Noun 이/가 되다: to become Noun

e.g. 꽃이 됐어요.
It became a flower.

제 딸이 어른이 됐어요.
My daughter became an adult.

저는 부자가 될 거예요. (부자 : a rich person)
I will become rich.

되다 does not have a direct antonym. To express negation, you simply add the negation adverb **안** before the verb. Therefore, the antonym of **되다** is **안 되다** (not become). We will explore this in more detail in the chapter on how to negate a verb.

Quiz

▶ TRACK 20

Fill in each blank with the correct particle and conjugation form.

1   제 친구는 의사 ☐ ☐ 요.

My friend became a doctor.

2   얼음 ☐ ☐ 거예요.

It will become ice.

ANSWER

1 가, 됐어   **2** 이, 될

to be good at or to be bad at

잘하다   **to be good at**

잘 is an adverb that means "well," so it literally means you do it well.

못하다   **to be bad at**

못 is an adverb that means "can't" or "poorly."

* 못하다 is pronounced as [모타다], following the consonant assimilation rule.

Both verbs are used with the 을/를. (This is because 하다 is a transitive verb, which can take an object. All transitive verbs can be used with the 을/를 particle.)

e.g.   게임을 잘해요. I'm good at games.

엄마는 요리를 잘해요. Mom is good at cooking.

운동을 못해요. I'm bad at sports.

제 친구는 한국어를 못해요. My friend can't speak Korean.

Quiz

▶ **TRACK 21**

Fill in the blank with the correct particle and verb.

1 노래 ☐ ☐ 요.
I'm good at singing.

2 제 친구는 운전 ☐ ☐ 요.
My friend is bad at driving.

ANSWER

1 를, 잘해   2 을, 못해

5   to go or to come

| 가다 | to go |

| 오다 | to come |

When 에 is used with the motion verbs **가다** and **오다**, it takes on the meaning of "to," indicating destination.

- Place Noun 에 가다: to go to Place
- Place Noun 에 오다: to come to Place

  e.g.   집에 가요.   Let's go (to) home.

         지윤이가 도서관에 갔어요.   Jiyun went to the library.

         엄마가 서울에 왔어요.   Mom came to Seoul.

Q   **I've seen 가다 used with 을/를 before. For example, instead of saying 학교에 가요, I've seen 학교를 가요. Is this grammatically incorrect?**

A.

While –에 가다 is the most grammatically correct expression, many Korean speakers do use 가다 and 오다 with 을/를 as well. This has become a habitual usage and is not strictly classified as incorrect. You can also choose to use none of these particles at all, and just use the place name followed by 가다 or 오다. (e.g. 학교 가요.)

Rather than strictly remembering that 가다 and 오다 must always be used with 에, it would be more helpful to know that while 에 is the most common and correct usage, it can sometimes be replaced with 을/를, or omitted entirely, and still be acceptable.

Quiz

1   Select the correct particle in the parentheses.

친구가 화장실(에 / 이) 갔어요.   (화장실: bathroom)

2   True or False

① 가다 means "to come" and 오다 means "to go."

☐ / ☐
TRUE   FALSE

② 가다 must always be used with 에 particle and not other particles.

☐ / ☐
TRUE   FALSE

ANSWER

1 에 (My friend went to the bathroom.)   **2** ① F ② F

1　Fill in the blank with the correct form of either 이다 or 아니다 in the
　　−요 ending 존댓말.

① 저는 학생 [　　　　]. 선생님 [　　　　].

I am not a student. I am a teacher.

② 포크 [　　　　]. 젓가락 [　　　　].

It's not a fork. It's a chopstick.

③ 고양이 [　　　　]. 여우 [　　　　].

It's not a cat. It's a fox.

2　Fill in the blank with the correct form of either 이/가 있다 or 없다 in the
　　−요 ending 존댓말.

① 사람 [　　　　].

There is a person. (= There's someone.)

② 동생 [　　　　].

I don't have a younger sibling.

③ 학교 [　　　　].

There is no school.

④ 차 [　　　　].

I have a car.

3　Fill in the blank with the correct form of 이/가 되다 in the −요 ending 존댓말.

① 제 친구는 가수 [　　　　].

My friend became a singer.

② 저는 행복한 사람 [　　　　].

I will become a happy person.

4   Fill in the blank with the correct form of either 을/를 잘하다 or 못하다 in the -요 ending 존댓말.

① 제 남편은 노래 [   ].

My husband is good at singing.

② 제 아내는 운동 [   ].

My wife is good at sports.

③ 한국어 [   ].

I'm not good at Korean.

④ 아빠는 요리 [   ].

My dad is bad at cooking.

5   Fill in the blank with the correct form of either 에 가다 or 오다 in the -요 ending 존댓말.

① 친구가 한국 [   ].

My friend will come to Korea.

② 헬스장 [   ].

Let's go to the gym.

ANSWER
1   ① (이) 아니에요, 이에요 ② (가) 아니에요, 이에요 ③ (가) 아니에요, 예요
2   ① 이 있어요 ② 이 없어요 ③ 가 없어요 ④ 가 있어요
3   ① 가 됐어요 ② 이 될 거예요
4   ① 를 잘해요 ② 을 잘해요 ③ 를 못해요 ④ 를 못해요
5   ① 에 올 거예요 ② 에 가요

How to say "Korean"

In English, there are adjectives that indicate something belongs to a specific country. For example, for things from Korea, you use "Korean" (e.g., Korean culture, Korean movies, Korean food). Similarly, for Spain, it's "Spanish"; for Italy, "Italian"; for Singapore, "Singaporean"; and for the UK, "British," among others.

However, in Korean, there aren't specific adjectives to indicate a particular country. Instead, you simply use the name of the country.

> e.g. Korean culture = 한국 문화 (literally, Korea + culture)
>
> Korean movies = 한국 영화 (Korea + movie)
>
> Korean food   = 한국 음식 (Korea + food)

If "Korean" refers to a person, you can say **한국 사람** or **한국인** (which literally means "Korea person"). For reference, **사람** and **인** both mean "person," with **사람** being a native Korean word and **인** being a Sino-Korean word.

* Sino-Korean words are derived from Chinese characters (Hanja).

For instance, "Korean" in "Korean friend" refers to a person, so you would say **한국인 친구**. You can also refer to a "Korean customer" as **한국인 손님**, Korean actor as **한국인 배우** and so on.

> e.g. Korean friend   = 한국인 친구 (or 한국 친구)
>
> Korean customer = 한국인 손님 (or 한국 손님)
>
> Korean actor   = 한국인 배우 (or 한국 배우)

It's also acceptable to just use the country name alone when referring to a person, so both forms are possible.

If "Korean" refers to the language, you can say **한국어** or **한국말** (which literally means "Korean language"). **어** and **말** both mean "language/talk/speech," with **어** being Sino-Korean and **말** being native Korean.

e.g.   Korean book = **한국어 책**

Korean class = **한국어 수업**

CHAPTER 6

에 & 에서
Place & Time Markers

In this chapter, we will learn about the meaning and usage of the Korean particles 에 and 에서. Although these two particles look similar, their usage is very different.

Do you remember from the previous chapter that 집에 있어요 means "I'm at home"? When 있다 is used with the particle 에, it indicates the current location of something or someone. This means that 에 functions as a location/place marker. Another particle 에서 also serves as a place marker, but they are used in different contexts. Let's explore how they are different.

(Before we begin, note that 에 and 에서 are particles whose form does not change, regardless of whether the noun they mark ends in a vowel or a consonant. In Korean, some particles change form depending on how the noun ends, while others do not. 에 and 에서 belong to the latter category.)

1 에 as a Place Marker

1. 에 + existence verb

When **에** is used as a place marker, the verb that follows should be related to "existence" rather than a specific action.

Generally, the two most common verbs with this meaning are **있다**(or **없다**) and **살다**.

> Place 에 있다 : to be at a place
>
> Place 에 없다 : to not be at a place
>
> Place 에 살다 : to live at a place

> *e.g.* 저는 학교에 있어요. I'm at school.
>
> 고양이가 집에 없어요. The cat isn't at home.
>
> 저는 한국에 살아요. I live in Korea.

Let's go a step further and learn the following pattern as well.

> Place 에 Noun 이/가 있다 : There's Noun at Place
>
> Place 에 Noun 이/가 없다 : There's no Noun at Place

This pattern is used to indicate whether something is present or absent in a specific place, and it usually starts with "Place에" at the beginning of the sentence.

> *e.g.* 제 방에 책상이 있어요. There's a desk in my room.
>
> 공원에 벤치가 없어요. There are no benches at a park.

Of course, the sentence can also start with Noun 이/가, with "Place에" coming afterward.

책상이 제 방에 있어요. The desk is in my room.

벤치가 공원에 없어요. The bench is not in the park.

Both of these are grammatically correct expressions. When 에 comes first, it indicates the general state of something being there, whereas when 이/가 comes first, it places more emphasis on the current state.

> **e.g.** 제 방에 책상이 있어요.
> There's a desk in my room. — It is usually the case.
>
> 책상이 제 방에 있어요.
> The desk is in my room. — It is currently the case.

The place marker 에 can also be followed by an action verb if that action causes an object or a body to exist on or within a certain place.

For example, consider verbs like 앉다 (to sit), 서다 (to stand), 놓다 (to place), and 넣다 (to put in). Let's take a closer look at each one.

- **앉다 (to sit)**: When you sit somewhere, your body (most likely your buttocks) comes to rest on that place. Therefore, you can use "place에 앉다" to express this. (e.g., 의자에 앉았어요. I sat on a chair.)

- **서다 (to stand)**: When you stand somewhere, your body ends up being present on that spot. Therefore, you can use "place에 서다" to express this. (e.g., 무대에 섰어요. I stood on a stage, or I was on stage.)

- **놓다 (to place)**: 놓다 is used when placing something on top of something else. When you place something on a surface, it naturally exists on that surface. Therefore, you can use "place에 놓다." (e.g., 책상에 펜을 놓았어요. I put the pen on the desk.)

- **넣다 (to put in)**: 넣다 is used when you put something inside something else. When you place something inside, it naturally exists within that space. Therefore, you can use "place에 넣다" (e.g., **가방에 책을 넣었어요**. I put the book in the bag.)

2. 에 + motion verb

As we learned in the previous chapter, the motion verbs **가다** (to go) and **오다** (to come) are used with **에** to indicate going or coming "to" a specific place. Since we've already covered this, let's jump straight into the examples.

> *e.g.* **매일 학교에 가요**. I go to school every day.
>
> **친구가 집에 갔어요.** My friend went home.
>
> **엄마가 한국에 올 거예요.** Mom will come to Korea.

2 ┃ 에서 as a Place Marker

When **에서** is used as a place marker, the verb that follows must be an <u>action verb</u>.

It can only be used in the context where a specific action is being performed at that location.

> *e.g.* **도서관에서 공부해요.** I study at the library.
>
> **침대에서 자요.** I sleep in (the) bed.
>
> **식당에서 밥을 먹었어요.** I had a meal at a restaurant.
>
> **학교에서 배웠어요.** I learned it at school.

One exception is the verb **살다**, which can be used with both **에** and **에서** to mark the place one lives. This is because **살다** can mean "to live" as in being alive, but it also implies the action of carrying out daily life. Therefore, when expressing where someone lives, both **에 살다** and **에서 살다** are correct.

> *e.g.* Teacher Vicky lives in Korea.
>
> **빅키 선생님은 한국에 살아요.**
>
> = **빅키 선생님은 한국에서 살아요.**

Q **Are 에 and 에서 like topic, subject, or object marking particles in that they can be omitted without affecting the meaning?**

A

No, **에** and **에서** cannot be omitted. While topic, subject, and object markers can often be omitted when the context makes it clear what the topic, subject, or object is, **에서** and **에** are different. If you omit these particles, the meaning becomes unclear or lost altogether, and the sentence may not make sense. Other than topic, subject, and object markers, particles must be used when necessary because omitting them can completely change or erase the intended meaning.

Quiz

Fill in the blank with the correct particle among 에 and 에서.

1 미국 [____] 살아요.
   I live in the US.

2 학교 [____] 한국어를 배워요.
   I learn Korean at school.

3 카페 [____] 친구를 만났어요.
   I met a friend in the café.

4 서점 [____] 책을 살 거예요.
   I will buy some books at a bookstore.

5 헬스장 [____] 있어요.
   I'm at the gym.

ANSWER

1 에 or 에서   **2** 에서   **3** 에서
4 에서   **5** 에

3 에 as a Time Marker

Unlike 에서, 에 can serve as a time marker as well. It marks time nouns to indicate what time it is currently or when exactly the action takes place.

(Although 에서 does have a function related to marking time, it is used to indicate a range rather than a specific point in time. We will explore this in more detail in the next chapter.)

Before we learn the usage of 에 as a time marker, let's first go over some of the most common time nouns.

1. Time Noun + 에

(1) Months

The names of the months in Korean are formed by combining the Sino-Korean number that represents the order of the month in the solar calendar with the Sino-Korean word 월 (which means "month").

For example, since January is the first month in the solar calendar, it is called **1월 (일월)** by combining the number **1 (일)** with **월**. February is **2월 (이월)**, March is **3월 (삼월)** and so on.

1월 (일월)	January	**7월 (칠월)**	July
2월 (이월)	February	**8월 (팔월)**	August
3월 (삼월)	March	**9월 (구월)**	September
4월 (사월)	April	**10월 (시월)**	October
5월 (오월)	May	**11월 (십일월)**	November
6월 (유월)	June	**12월 (십이월)**	December

(2) Days of the Week

일요일 : Sunday

월요일 : Monday

화요일 : Tuesday

수요일 : Wednesday

목요일 : Thursday

금요일 : Friday

토요일 : Saturday

You may have noticed that all these words end with 요일. 일 is a Sino-Korean word that means "day," and 요일 represents the days of the week.

The words used for each day (e.g., 일, 월, 화, 수) are derived from celestial bodies (the sun and moon) and the five natural elements (fire, water, wood, metal, and earth).

(3) Time of the Day

아침 : morning

오후 : afternoon

저녁 : evening

밤 : night

(4) Seasons

봄: spring	여름: summer	가을: fall, autumn	겨울: winter

Now, let's look at some sentences using these time nouns with 에.

> *e.g.* **3월에 이사 갈 거예요.**
> I will move out in March.
>
> **8월에 여름방학이에요.**
> It's summer vacation in August.
>
> **일요일에 집에서 쉬었어요.**
> I rested at home on Sunday.
>
> **저녁에 버스에서 음악을 들어요.**
> I listen to music on the bus in the evening.
>
> **여름에 비가 많이 와요.**
> It rains a lot in summer.

Easy, right? As you can see, 에 functions as a time marker used to pinpoint "when" something happens.

Did you by any chance notice in the third and fourth examples what we've covered in Chapter 1? In the first chapter, I briefly mentioned the basic word order in Korean, and when both time and place information appear in a sentence, the common order is to mention the time first, followed by the place.

> *e.g.* **일요일에 집에서 쉬어요.**
>   time   place
>
> **저녁에 버스에서 음악을 들어요.**
>   time   place

Of course, switching the word order of these two elements doesn't make the sentence grammatically incorrect. Both phrases function as adverbs, adding details to the verb. This means they can appear in any order before the verb without breaking grammatical rules.

But taking this as a general rule of thumb will help you avoid getting stuck with word order when constructing more detailed sentences.

2. Time Adverbs

One important thing to note is that **에** can only mark time *nouns*, not adverbs.

There are some time adverbs that are often mixed up with time nouns. The most common examples are:

> **어제**: yesterday
>
> **오늘**: today
>
> **내일**: tomorrow
>
> **매일**: every day

These words are adverbs that already indicate "at" a specific time, so you cannot add **에** to them.

e.g. I read a book yesterday.	**어제 책을 읽었어요.**	(O)
	어제에 책을 읽었어요.	(×)
I work today.	**오늘 일해요.**	(O)
	오늘에 일해요.	(×)
I will work out tomorrow.	**내일 운동할 거예요.**	(O)
	내일에 운동할 거예요.	(×)
I drink tea every day.	**매일 차를 마셔요.**	(O)
	매일에 차를 마셔요.	(×)

Quiz

1 Select the correct particle in the parentheses.

아침(에 / 에서) 일어나요.

I wake up in the morning.

2 Fill in each blank with the correct particle.

목요일 ☐ 옷 가게 ☐ 옷을 샀어요.

I bought some clothes on Thursday in the clothing shop.

3 Select the grammatically INCORRECT sentence.

① 봄에 벚꽃을 봤어요. (벚꽃: cherry blossom)

② 내일에 공원에서 친구를 만날 거예요. (공원: park)

③ 월요일에 회사에서 일할 거예요. (회사: company, office, workplace)

ANSWER

1 에

2 에, 에서

3 ② 내일에 친구를 만날 거예요 - I will meet a friend at the park tomorrow. (에 should be removed.)
　① 봄에 벚꽃을 봤어요. - I saw cherry blossoms in the spring.
　③ 월요일에 회사에서 일할 거예요. - I will work at the office on Monday.

1 **True or False**

① Both 에 and 에서 can be used with the verb 살다.

☐ / ☐
TRUE FALSE

② You can use both 에 and 에서 as a time marker to indicate when something's happening.

☐ / ☐
TRUE FALSE

③ When 에서 is used as a place marker, it should be followed by an action verb.

☐ / ☐
TRUE FALSE

④ When 에 functions as a time marker, it can be attached not only to time nouns but also to time adverbs like 오늘 and 내일.

☐ / ☐
TRUE FALSE

⑤ In a Korean sentence, it's more common to mention the time before the place when giving both pieces of information.

☐ / ☐
TRUE FALSE

2 **Fill in each blank with the correct particle.**

① 지하철역 ⬚ 있어요.

I'm at a subway station.

② 저희 동네 ⬚ 은행 ⬚ 있어요.

There's a bank in my neighborhood.

③ 차 ⬚ 있어요.

I have a car.

④ 카페 ⬚ 커피를 마셔요.

I drink coffee at a café.

⑤ 오후 ⬚ 헬스장 ⬚ 갔어요.

I went to the gym in the afternoon.

3   Select the correctly translated sentence.

(1) There is no flower in the park.

① 공원에서 꽃을 없어요.   ② 공원에 꽃이 없어요.

③ 공원에 꽃을 없어요.   ④ 공원에서 꽃이 없어요.

(2) I don't have cash.

① 현금이 없어요.   ② 현금을 없어요.

③ 현금에 없어요.   ④ 현금에서 없어요.

(3) I read a book at the library.

① 도서관에 책을 읽어요.   ② 도서관에 책이 읽어요.

③ 도서관에서 책이 읽어요.   ④ 도서관에서 책을 읽어요.

4   Translate the following sentences in the –요 ending 존댓말.

① I wear a coat in the winter. (코트: coat)

_____

② I will rest at home tomorrow.

_____

③ I bought a book at a bookstore yesterday. (서점: bookstore)

_____

④ I learn Korean at school on the weekend.

_____

⑤ I watched a movie at the movie theater on Saturday. (영화관: movie theater)

_____

ANSWER

1   ① T ② F ③ T ④ F ⑤ T   2   ① 에 ② 에, 이 ③ 가 ④ 에서 ⑤ 에, 에

3   (1) ② (2) ① (3) ④

4   ① 겨울에 코트를 입어요. ② 내일 집에서 쉴 거예요. ③ 어제 서점에서 책을 샀어요.
     ④ 주말에 학교에서 한국어를 배워요. ⑤ 토요일에 영화관에서 영화를 봤어요.

콩글리쉬(Konglish)

Do you remember the word **헬스장** that we learned in this chapter? It means "gym."

If you break it down, **헬스** comes from the English word "health," which is transliterated into Korean, and the Sino-Korean word **장**, means "place." So **헬스장** literally translates to a place for health, or simply, a gym.

There are quite a few Korean words influenced by English, known as Konglish (Korean + English), which includes Koreanized English words or a mixture of English and Korean words.

Let's take a look at some of the most common Konglish words.

- **핸드폰** (cellphone): This word is made by combining **핸드** from the English word "hand" and **폰** from "phone." You can also just say **폰** (phone) as well.

- **셀카** (selfie): It's a shortened form of **셀프 카메라** (self camera), which refers to a selfie.

- **룸메** (roommate): While the full word **룸메이트** (roommate) is also used, it's often shortened to **룸메**. It refers to someone you live with or share your apartment/flat with.

- **원룸** (studio apartment): This refers to a small apartment with only one room, which is known in English as a "studio apartment."

- **원샷** (bottoms up): "One-shot" is a Konglish term used in drinking culture, meaning to drink a glass in one go. In English, similar expressions would be "bottoms up" or "take it in one go." In English, "one shot" refers to a single attempt or a single bullet, but in Korean, it's mostly used in the context of drinking.

- **아르바이트** (part-time job): Borrowed from the German word "Arbeit," it corresponds to "part-time job" in English. Although this isn't Konglish, it's still a word influenced by a Western language.

CHAPTER 7

부터, 에서 & 까지
Particles for
Marking a Range

In this chapter, you'll learn the specific usages of the three particles 부터, 에서, and 까지 and how they are used to mark a range.

1 부터

The usage of **부터**, **에서**, and **까지** can be easily understood by looking at the examples below:

| time | A**부터** B**까지** : from A to B |

| location | A**에서** B**까지** : from A to B |

까지 is used to mark the end of any range, whether it's time, location, price, or anything else.

On the other hand, **부터** and **에서** mark the start of a range. They can sometimes be interchangeable, but their usage differs slightly.

부터 usually marks the starting point in a **time range**.

e.g. **월요일부터 금요일까지** from Monday to Friday

일요일	월요일	화요일	수요일	목요일	금요일	토요일

월요일부터 금요일까지 일해요. I work from Monday to Friday.

3월부터 5월까지 from March to May

1월	2월	3월	4월	5월	6월

3월부터 5월까지 봄이에요. It's spring from March to May.

However, its usage isn't limited to time ranges alone.

부터 can also be used with nouns that have nothing to do with time. In this case, it means you did that noun first when performing the action. Depending on the context, it could be translated as "first" or "starting with."

e.g. **한글부터 배웠어요.**
I first learned Hangeul. (I started learning with Hangeul.)

샐러드부터 먹어요.
Let's have the salad first. (Let's start eating with salad.)

스트레칭부터 시작했어요.
I started with stretching. (시작하다: to start)

2 에서

에서 usually marks the starting point in a **place range**.

e.g. 집에서 학교까지 from home to school

집에서 학교까지 얼마나 걸려요?

How long does it take from home to school?

여기에서 저기까지 from here to there

여기에서 저기까지 어떻게 가요?

How do you get from here to there?

VOCAB

여기 here (close to the speaker)
거기 there (close to the listener or referring to a place the speaker is thinking of)
저기 over there (far from both the speaker and the listener)
어떻게 how
얼마나 how long, how much

There isn't a strict rule that 부터 must always be used for location ranges and 에서 must always be used for time ranges. There are instances where both 부터 and 에서 can be used for location and time ranges.
(e.g., 월요일에서 금요일까지, 여기부터 저기까지)

However, 부터 is more often used for time ranges, and 에서 for location ranges. So it would be more helpful and easier to remember them this way, though the reverse usage is also acceptable.

에서 is also often used when talking about approximate figures, not just time ranges.

e.g. 천 원에서 이천 원 정도

around 1,000 won to 2,000 won

제 키는 170에서 172 센티 정도예요.

My height is around 170 to 172cm.

VOCAB

원 won (Korean currecny)
정도 around, approximately
키 height   센티(미터) cm

3 까지

까지 marks the endpoint of any range, including both time and location. It can also indicate a deadline or boundary. It is often translated as "until" or "by (deadline)."

> e.g. 끝까지 until the end
>
> 끝까지 갈 거예요. I will make it till the end.
>
> 내일까지 끝낼 거예요. I will finish it by tomorrow.
> 10쪽까지 읽었어요. I read up to page 10.

VOCAB
끝 end
끝내다 to finish

Quiz

Fill in the blank with the correct particle.

1 토요일 ⬚ 월요일 ⬚ 쉴 거예요. (쉬다: to rest)

   I will rest from Saturday to Monday.

2 학교 ⬚ 버스 정류장 ⬚ 얼마나 걸려요?

   How long does it take from school to the bus stop?

3 책 ⬚ 읽었어요.

   I read the book first.

ANSWER
1 부터, 까지   2 에서, 까지   3 부터

130   CHAPTER 7   부터, 에서 & 까지 PARTICLES FOR MARKING A RANGE

1 Fill in the blank with the correct particles.

① 금요일 [　　　　] 일요일 [　　　　] 여행했어요.
I traveled from Friday to Sunday.

② 서울 [　　　　] 부산 [　　　　] 얼마나 걸려요?
How long does it take from Seoul to Busan?

③ 제 방 [　　　　] 치웠어요.
I cleaned my room first.

④ 저녁 [　　　　] 끝낼 거예요.
I will finish it by the evening.

⑤ 오천 원 [　　　　] 육천 원 정도예요.
It's around 5,000 to 6,000 won.

2 Translate the following sentences in the −요 ending 존댓말.

① How do you get from here to there?

_____

② It's summer from June to August.

_____

③ I will start from tomorrow.

_____

④ I watched the movie until the end.

_____

⑤ How long does it take from the airport to the hotel? (airport: 공항, hotel: 호텔)

_____

ANSWER

1　① 부터, 까지　② 에서, 까지　③ 부터　④ 까지　⑤ 에서

2　① 여기에서 저기까지 어떻게 가요?　② 6월부터 8월까지 여름이에요.
　　③ 내일부터 시작할 거예요.　④ 영화를 끝까지 봤어요.　⑤ 공항에서 호텔까지 얼마나 걸려요?

CHAPTER 8

에게/한테
to and from someone

In this chapter, you will learn about the meaning and usage of 에게 and 한테. These two particles have the same meaning and are interchangeable.

The first thing to note about 에게 and 한테 is that these particles **can only be used with nouns referring to people or animals**. They are not used with inanimate objects or things that do not move around with legs.

에게 and 한테 have exactly the same meaning and are always interchangeable. The difference is that 한테 is more colloquial, so you'll hear it more often in everyday conversations, whereas 에게 is more commonly used in writing.

These particles have two main meanings:
① to and ② from.

This means they can be used ① <u>when performing an action toward a specific person ("to")</u> or ② <u>when receiving an action from that person ("from").</u>

1 to [person]

One of the most common actions performed toward someone is "giving." Remember that in Korean, "to give" is the verb 주다?

First, let's look at some sentences where 주다 is used with 에게/한테.

> *e.g.* **엄마에게 선물을 줬어요**.
>
> I gave a gift to mom.

친구한테 책을 줬어요.

I gave a book to my friend.

고양이에게 밥을 줬어요.

I gave some food to a cat.

Pairing 에게/한테 with 주다 can actually feel a bit counterintuitive sometimes, especially for learners whose native language is English.

For example, consider the following English sentences:

I gave mom a gift.

I gave my friend a book.

In English, when you give something to someone, you can use "someone" ("mom" or "my friend" in the case of examples) as the object of the verb "give" without adding the preposition "to." Because of this, beginners often intuitively feel that "mom" and "my friend" are the direct objects of 주다 (to give) and might make the mistake of saying,

엄마를 선물을 줬어요. (×)

친구를 책을 줬어요. (×)

and incorrectly use the object marker 을/를 with "someone."

However, in Korean, when you give something to a person, you always need to use 에게/한테. The people who receive what you're giving CANNOT be objects of 주다 (to give).

Please keep this in mind when constructing sentences involving giving actions.

Quiz

▶ TRACK 26

Select the correct particle in the parentheses.

그 사람(한테 / 을) 제 번호를 줄 거예요.

I will give that person my number.

ANSWER
한테

Aside from **주다**, there are quite a few Korean verbs that function in a similar way. It's easier to understand if you think about actions directed toward a person.

Some common verbs include:

❶ **말하다** to tell

❷ **전화하다** to call [phone call]

❸ **보내다** to send

❹ **가르치다** to teach

❺ **물어보다** to ask

These verbs are often used with **에게/한테** to indicate who the recipient/target of the action is.

e.g. ❶ **말하다** to tell

친구들한테 **말했어요**.

I told my friends.

❷ **전화하다** to call

매일 가족에게 **전화해요**.

I call my family every day.

❸ **보내다** to send

선생님한테 **이메일을 보냈어요**.

I sent an email to the teacher.

남편에게 **편지를 보냈어요**.

I sent a letter to my husband.

❹ **가르치다** to teach

저는 학생들에게 **한국어를 가르쳐요**.

I teach Korean to the students.

With **가르치다** (to teach), it's actually okay to use **을/를** to mark the person being taught.

For example, you can say,

저는 아이들을 가르쳐요. I teach children.

However, when both the person and the subject being taught appear in the same sentence, the person must be marked with **에게/한테**, and the subject with **을/를**.

For instance, you CANNOT say,

저는 학생들을 한국어를 가르쳐요. (×)
— it should be **학생들에게/한테**.

Q **What is 들 in 학생들 and 아이들? Is it a plural suffix?**

A

Yes, that's correct. You might have noticed **들** in example sentences, such as **학생들** (students) and **아이들** (children), where **학생** (student) and **아이** (child) are combined with **들** to form the plural.

Another thing to note is that unlike English, Korean isn't very strict about plural forms. So when referring to general concepts, you can often just use the singular form (e.g., "I love babies" can be **저는 아기를 좋아해요** instead of **아기들을**).

You can use **들** when you specifically want to indicate more than one person or refer to specific people.

❺ **물어보다** to ask
현지인들에게 길을 물어봤어요.
I asked the locals for directions.

부모님한테 물어봤어요?
Did you ask your parents?

Quiz

Fill in each blank with the correct particle.

1 제 친구 [____] 비밀 [____] 말했어요.

I told my secret to my friend.

2 부모님 [____] 매일 전화해요.

I call my parents every day.

3 학생들 [____] 메일* [____] 보냈어요.

I sent my students an email.

> * 메일 and 이메일 both mean "email." Remember that 메 is spelled with ㅔ, not ㅐ.

4 엄마는 학교 [____] 아이들 [____] 영어 [____] 가르쳐요.

Mom teaches English to children at school.

ANSWER

1 에게 or 한테, 을   **2** 에게 or 한테
3 에게 or 한테, 을   **4** 에서, 에게 or 한테, 를

2 from [person]

Interestingly, **에게/한테** can mean not only "to" but also its opposite, "from."

When it means "from," it will naturally be used verbs that convey the meaning of receiving an action.

One verb that probably comes to your mind first would be **받다** (to receive).

> e.g. **친구한테 선물을 받았어요.**
> I received a gift from my friend.
>
> **남자친구한테 청혼을 받았어요.**
> I received a proposal from
> my boyfriend.

In addition to **받다**, other verbs commonly used with **에게/한테** (from) are:

❶ **듣다** to listen, to hear

❷ **배우다** to learn

❸ **빌리다** to borrow

Let's look at example sentences for each of these verbs.

> e.g. ❶ **듣다** to listen, hear
> **엄마에게 좋은 소식을 들었어요.**
> I heard some good news from mom.
>
> **누구한테 들었어요?** (누구: who)
> Whom did you hear it from?
>
> ❷ **배우다** to learn
> **빅키 선생님한테 한국어를 배웠어요.**
> I learned Korean from Teacher Vicky.
>
> ❸ **빌리다** to borrow
> **친구한테 신발을 빌렸어요.**
> I borrowed shoes from my friend.

에게서/한테서

In most cases, whether **에게/한테** means "to" or "from" can be easily understood from the context, especially based on the verb that follows. So it's perfectly fine to use the same form for both meanings.

However, if you want to emphasize the "from" meaning, you can add **서** to make it **에게서/한테서**.

Both **에게/한테** and **에게서/한테서** convey the meaning of "from" and grammatically correct, but **에게/한테** is still more common.

> *e.g.* 엄마에게서 좋은 소식을 들었어요.
> I heard some good news from mom.
>
> 빅키 선생님한테서 한국어를 배웠어요.
> I learned Korean from Teacher Vicky.
>
> 친구한테서 신발을 빌렸어요.
> I borrowed shoes from my friend.

Please note that **에게서/한테서** only means "from" and not "to".

Quiz

▶ TRACK 28

Select the correct meaning of **에게/한테** in each sentence.

1 친구한테 물어봤어요. (to / from)

2 지수 씨한테 옷을 빌렸어요. (to / from)

3 딸한테 전화했어요. (to / from)

4 한국어를 누구에게 배웠어요? (to / from)

ANSWER

1 to   **2** from   **3** to   **4** from

3 께 - Honorific

In Korean, there is something called "honorifics," which are used to show respect toward the person being referred to in the sentence.

Honorifics are a slightly different concept from 존댓말 (polite speech), though they can be considered a part of 존댓말. While 존댓말 is mainly distinguished by sentence endings, honorifics involve specific particles and altered forms of verbs and adjectives.

We'll explore Korean honorifics in greater detail in *Korean Grammar Palette for Beginners 2*.

For now, as a first step, let's learn about the honorific form of 에게/한테, which is 께.

It carries both the meanings of "to" and "from."

> *e.g.* **부모님께 매일 전화해요.**
> I call my parents every day.
>
> **선생님께 이메일을 보냈어요.**
> I sent an email to the teacher.
>
> **빅키 선생님께 한국어를 배웠어요.**
> I learned Korean from Teacher Vicky.

It would sound quite awkward to use 께 when referring to someone like a close friend or spouse.

For example,

> **친구께** (×) → **친구한테** (O)
> **남편께** (×) → **남편에게** (O)

Another important thing to note is that when **에게/한테** means "from," you add **서** to form **에게서/한테서**, but this rule does not apply to honorifics. You should not use **께서** to indicate "from" in the honorific form. **께서** is actually a completely different honorific particle with a different meaning.

Q **Then what does 께서 mean?**

A

께 and 께서 look very similar, so they can easily be mixed up or mistaken for the same particle. However, 께 means "to/from," while 께서 is the honorific form of the subject marker 이/가.

For example,

선생님께서 저에게 주셨어요.

The teacher gave it to me.

선생님께 드렸어요.

I gave it to the teacher.

* 주시다 and 드리다 are the honorific forms of the verb 주다.

Quiz

True or False

1   에게/한테's honorific form is 께.

    ☐ TRUE / ☐ FALSE

2   께 means both "to" and "from" a person.

    ☐ TRUE / ☐ FALSE

3   께서 means "from."

    ☐ TRUE / ☐ FALSE

ANSWER

1 T **2** T **3** F

4 에 for Non-humans

We've learned that **에게/한테** can only be used with people or sometimes with animal nouns. A more accurate explanation would be that it is generally used with people, but it can also apply to anything you wish to personify.

When it comes to pets, we often treat them like members of the family. That's why using **에게/한테** with pets feels natural.

However, if it's not an animal you want to personify, using **에** is the correct choice. This applies to all non-human nouns—such as inanimate objects, insects, or plants—where **에** is more appropriate to indicate "to" or "from."

e.g. **나무에 물을 줬어요.**

I watered the tree.

손가락이 칼에 베였어요.

My finger was cut by a knife.

모기에 물렸어요.

I got bitten by a mosquito.

뱀에 물렸어요.

I got bitten by a snake.

VOCAB
베이다 to be cut   물리다 to be bitten

Quiz

▶ TRACK 29

Fill in the blank with the correct particle.

1 꽃 ⬚ 물을 줬어요. (꽃: flower)

2 벌레 ⬚ 물렸어요. (벌레: bug)

ANSWER

1 에 2 에

1 Select the TWO particles below that are used to mean "to/from [person]."

① 에서   ② 에게   ③ 에   ④ 한테

2 Match the following verbs with their correct meanings.

① 주다 •   • to tell

② 받다 •   • to give

③ 말하다 •   • to listen

④ 듣다 •   • to receive

⑤ 가르치다 •   • to call

⑥ 배우다 •   • to borrow

⑦ 전화하다 •   • to teach

⑧ 빌리다 •   • to learn

3 Fill in each blank with the correct particle.

① 누구[⬚] 줬어요? Whom did you give it to?

② 선생님[⬚] 받았어요. I received it from my teacher.

③ 부모님[⬚] 말했어요? Did you tell your parents?

④ 친구[⬚] 빌렸어요. I borrowed it from a friend.

⑤ 남동생이 벌레[⬚] 물렸어요.

My younger brother got bitten by a bug.

4 **Translate each sentence in the –요 ending 존댓말.**

① I will call my boyfriend tomorrow.

_____

② I gave water to a cat. / I gave the cat water.

_____

③ Did you water the tree?

_____

④ I learned cooking from my older sister.
  (= I learned how to cook from my older sister.)

  [요리: cooking, 언니: older sister (for female), 누나: older sister (for male)]

_____

⑤ I asked the child their name.

_____

⑥ Mom teaches English to students.

_____

ANSWER

1 ②, ④

2 ① to give ② to receive ③ to tell ④ to listen ⑤ to teach ⑥ to learn ⑦ to call ⑧ to borrow

3 ① 에게 or 한테 ② 에게(서), 한테(서) or 께 ③ 에게, 한테 or 께
  ④ 에게(서) or 한테(서) ⑤ 에

4 ① 내일 남자친구에게/한테 전화할 거예요.
  ② 고양이에게/한테 물을 줬어요.
  ③ 나무에 물을 줬어요?
  ④ 언니에게(서)/한테(서) 요리를 배웠어요. or 누나에게(서)/한테(서) 요리를 배웠어요.
  ⑤ 아이에게/한테 이름을 물어봤어요.
  ⑥ 엄마는 학생들에게/한테 영어를 가르쳐요.

밥 vs. 음식? 먹다 vs. 밥을 먹다?
What is the difference?

Korea has a long history where wealth was rare, especially among the common people, who often lived in poverty. Because of this, having regular meals for survival has historically been very important. This cultural value has continued into modern times, where people often start conversations by asking if the other person has eaten.

The word most commonly used in this context is **밥**.
밥 actually has two meanings:

> 1. cooked rice
>
> 2. meal (as in, breakfast, lunch or dinner)

When a Korean friend asks, "**밥 먹었어요?**" or "**밥 드셨어요?**"
(**드시다** is the honorific form of **먹다**), they may be genuinely curious if you've eaten, but in most cases, it's just a polite way of asking how you're doing. Historically, people would ask if someone had eaten to check on their well-being, and this practice has carried over into modern times.

The word that directly corresponds to "food" is **음식**,
but **밥을 먹다** is much more commonly used than **음식을 먹다**,
except in cases where you specifically need to emphasize the word **음식**.
This is why even when feeding animals or pets, the word **밥** is used.

For example,

> ### 고양이에게 밥을 줬어요.
> I fed the cat. (I gave food to the cat.)
>
> ### 강아지에게 매일 밥을 줘요.
> I feed my dog every day.

There is a more specific term for food meant for animals, which is **사료**.

For example, **고양이 사료** means "cat food," and **강아지 사료** means "dog food." But **사료** is often replaced with **밥** in everyday conversations.

밥을 먹다 is a native Korean word, and there is a Sino-Korean synonym with the exact same meaning, which is 식사하다.

This means you can interchangeably use "밥 먹었어요?" with "식사했어요?," and "밥 드셨어요?" with "식사하셨어요?"(the honorific form).

So, the next time you bump into a Korean friend or acquaintance on the street, instead of saying "안녕/안녕하세요!," why not try greeting them with "밥 먹었어(요)?" or "식사했어(요)?"

CHAPTER 9

와/과, (이)랑, 하고 & (으)로
More Essential Particles (1)

In this chapter, you will learn four more basic particles. Each particle has more than one meaning, and we will explore the different meanings each particle conveys and how they are specifically used.

1 와/과, (이)랑, 하고 - "and" and "with"

These three particles —와/과, (이)랑, and 하고— are grouped together because they are always interchangeable and share the same meaning.

These particles have two meanings. Let's take a closer look at each one.

1. and

The first meaning is "and."

와/과, (이)랑 and 하고 are particles, so they can only be used with **nouns**. They cannot be used as "and" to connect verbs or sentences.

For example, they can certainly be used in phrases like,

- fruits **and** vegetables
- students **and** a teacher
- a cat **and** a dog
- English **and** Korean

because the "and" is used for connecting nouns.

However, they are not used to connect other parts of speech, like in the sentences

- I went grocery shopping **and** watched a movie.
- I feel sleepy **and** tired.

This type of "and" is called a conjunction, and we'll learn more about it in *Korean Grammar Palette for Beginners 2*. For now, let's focus on how to use "and" as a particle to connect two or more nouns.

(1) 와/과

Among these three particles, **와/과** sounds the most formal, so it is generally used more in written language than in spoken language. However, that doesn't mean it can't be used in spoken language.

If the preceding noun ends with a consonant, you use **과**, and if it ends with a vowel, you use **와**.

> **Preceding Noun ends with a consonant: Noun 과**

> **Preceding Noun ends with a vowel: Noun 와**

(Usually, particles beginning with a vowel are used when the preceding noun ends with a consonant. However, this case is different, so you can note it as an exception.)

과일과 채소 fruits and vegetables

학생들과 선생님 students and a teacher

고양이와 강아지 a cat and a dog

영어와 한국어 English and Korean

e.g. 과일과 채소를 좋아해요.

I like fruits and vegetables.

학생들과 선생님이 학교에 있어요.

The students and a teacher are at school.

고양이와 강아지를 키워요.*

I raise a cat and a dog.

* In Korean, instead of saying "have a pet" using 있다, it's more common
to say "raise a pet" using 키우다 (to raise).

영어와 한국어를 해요.*

I speak English and Korean.

* When saying "speak a language," you can simply use the verb
하다 for "speak." While 하다 generally means "to do," if the object is
a language, it naturally translates to "speak."

(2) (이)랑

Preceding Noun ends with a consonant: Noun 이랑

Preceding Noun ends with a vowel: Noun 랑

과일이랑 채소
학생들이랑 선생님
고양이랑 강아지
영어랑 한국어

(3) 하고

Among the three particles, this one is the most straightforward and simple. It doesn't depend on the form of the noun; regardless of what noun comes before it, you just use **하고**.

> 과일하고 채소
> 학생들하고 선생님
> 고양이하고 강아지
> 영어하고 한국어

2. with [someone]

In this usage, it can only be used with person nouns (or animals you want to personify.) It's used to express that a specific action was done with a particular person or group of people.

e.g. 친구들과 놀았어요.
친구들이랑 놀았어요.
친구들하고 놀았어요.
I hung out with my friends.

원어민과 대화했어요.
원어민이랑 대화했어요.
원어민하고 대화했어요.
I conversed with a native speaker.

남자친구와 저녁을 먹었어요.
남자친구랑 저녁을 먹었어요.
남자친구하고 저녁을 먹었어요.
I had dinner with my boyfriend.

엄마와 영화를 볼 거예요.

엄마랑 영화를 볼 거예요.

엄마하고 영화를 볼 거예요.

I will watch a movie with my mom.

Quiz

▶ TRACK 30

Fill in the blank with the correct word and particle.

1 　　　　　　　　 문화를 좋아해요. (Use 와/과.)

I like Korean food and culture.

2 헬스장에서 　　　　　　　　 운동했어요. (Use (이)랑.)

I worked out with my friends at the gym.

3 　　　　　　　　 영어를 알아요. (Use (이)랑.)

I know Korean and English.

4 　　　　　　　　 병원에 갔어요. (Use 하고.)

I went to the hospital with my mom.

ANSWER

1 한국 음식과　2 친구들이랑
3 한국어랑　4 엄마하고

2 (으)로

(으)로 is also one of the essential and basic Korean particles, with a wide range of uses.

Before we dive into the specific meanings, let's first learn how to use (으)로 grammatically.

As you might have guessed, if the noun marked by (으)로 ends in a consonant, you use 으로. If it ends in a vowel, you use 로.

> **Preceding Noun ends with a consonant :** Noun **으로**

> **Preceding Noun ends with a vowel :** Noun **로**

1. Direction

One of (으)로's key functions is indicating direction, and it can be used with these six main direction nouns.

위 = up

아래 / 밑 = down

오른쪽 = right(오른 = right, 쪽 = side)

왼쪽 = left(왼 = left)

앞 = front

뒤 = back

e.g. 오른쪽으로 가. Go right. (or, Go to the right side.)

왼쪽으로 와. Come left. (or, Come to the left side.)

앞으로 가. Go forward.

뒤로 와. Come backward.

위로 올라와. Come up.

위로 올라가. Go up.

아래로 내려와. Come down.

밑으로 내려가. Go down.

> VOCAB
> 올라오다 to come up
> 올라가다 to go up
> 내려오다 to come down
> 내려가다 to go down

2. Destination

(으)로 can also be used to mark the specific location you're headed to.

In the previous chapter, we learned that the particle 에 can also express the same thing when used with motion verbs, like 가다 and 오다.

Both 에 and (으)로 can be used to express "to (a place)," but they have a slightly different nuance.

(으)로 vs. 에

에 is used when the focus is only on the destination—the place where someone is going.

(으)로 not only points to the destination but also suggests that the person is moving from one place to another. It adds the idea of a starting point.

Let's start with some examples using 에:

저는 매일 학교에 가요.

I go to school every day.

엄마가 잠깐 화장실에 갔어요.

Mom went to the bathroom for a moment.

Here, **에** is used because the focus is on the specific place you go everyday (**학교**, school) and where Mom went (**화장실**, the bathroom).

Now, let's compare two sentences that use **에** and **(으)로** to see how they are different.

어디에 가? (= 어디 가?)*

Where are you going?

어디로 가요?

Where do we go (from here)?

* 어디 means "where," and 어디에 (to where) can often be shortened to just 어디.

When you ask **어디에 가?**, you're specifically asking about the destination—where you are heading—without considering the starting point.

On the other hand, when you ask **어디로 가요?** you're not just asking where they are going, but it also suggests that you are moving from one location (starting point) to another location (destination.)

Typically, you would specify the starting point using **에서** and then indicate where you're headed with **(으)로** (e.g., **여기에서 저기로**, **학교에서 집으로**). However, if it's clear from the context where the starting point is, you can omit mentioning it and just use **(으)로** alone.

To sum up:

- Use **에** when you're just talking about the <u>destination</u>. It is rarely used with a starting point.

- Use **(으)로** when you want to indicate the direction of movement from one place to another. The starting point is marked with **에서**, but if the starting point is obvious from the context, there's no need to include it.

e.g. 저는 경기도에서 서울로 통근해요.

I commute from Gyeonggi Province to Seoul.

버스 정류장에서 지하철역으로 갔어요.

I went from the bus stop to the subway station.

저는 (여기서)* 호텔로 돌아갈 거예요.

I will go back to the hotel (from here.)

* 에서 is commonly shortened to 서, especially when it's combined with 여기(here), 거기(there) and 저기(over there) — becoming 여기서(from here), 거기서(from there), and 저기서(from over there.)

Q What exactly is the difference between "~에서 ~까지" and "~에서 ~(으)로"?

A

~에서 ~까지 indicates the range itself, regardless of movement. It expresses the span or distance between two points.

On the other hand, ~에서 ~(으)로 is used when indicating the direction of movement from the starting point to the destination.

For example:

서울에서 부산까지 갔어요.

I went from Seoul to Busan.

→ This indicates that you traveled the entire distance between Seoul and Busan.

서울에서 부산으로 갔어요.

I went from Seoul to Busan.

→ This indicates that the direction of your movement was to Busan from Seoul.

Quiz

1 Select the correct word/particle in the parentheses.

ⓘ (왼쪽 / 오른쪽)으로 가.

Turn right.

② 앞(으로 / 에서) 와요.

Come forward.

③ 어디(로 / 에)가요?

Where do we go from here?

④ 한국(으로 / 에서) 미국(으로 / 에) 돌아갈 거예요.

We will go back to the US from Korea.

2 Which particle would you use if you intend to emphasize the direction of movement rather than the range?

뒤에서 앞(까지 / 으로) 밀어.

Push it from the back to the front.

ANSWER
1 ① 오른쪽 ② 으로 ③ 로 ④ 에서, 으로
2 으로

3. A Means of Transportation / Tool

(으)로 can also be used to indicate how you travel (like by bus or train) or what you use to perform an action (like with a pencil or any kind of tool).

(1) Means of Transportation – Translates as "by"

When you want to specify the means of transportation you use to get from one place to another, you can use (으)로 to mean "by."

버스로 가요.

Let's go by bus.

기차로 여행했어요.

I traveled by train.

저는 지하철로 출퇴근해요.

I commute by subway.

VOCAB

Means of Transportation

자전거 bicycle   지하철 subway
버스 bus   기차 train
차 car   택시 taxi
배 ship   비행기 airplane

When the noun that (으)로 marks ends with the final consonant ㄹ, you shouldn't add 으 and just use 로.

> *e.g.* 지하철으로 (x), 지하철로 (o)

(2) Tools – Translates as "with"

You can also use (으)로 to show what tool or object you used to do something. In this case, it means "with."

Make sure to note that (으)로 means "with" in a different way than 와/과, (이)랑, or 하고. When these three particles mean "with," they are only used with a noun that refers to people, while (으)로 is used when you're talking about using inanimate objects or even body parts as tools.

> *e.g.* 손으로 편지를 썼어요.
>
> I wrote a letter with my hand. (I hand-wrote the letter myself.)
>
> 이건 종이로 만들었어요.
>
> I made it with paper.
>
> 연필로 썼어요.
>
> I wrote it with a pencil.
>
> 가위로 종이를 잘랐어요.
>
> I cut the paper with scissors.

You can also use (으)로 to express speaking in a specific language.

e.g. **친구랑 한국어로 대화했어요.**
I conversed in Korean with my friend.

영어로 해요.
Let's speak in English.

Q **한국어를 해요 vs. 한국어로 해요, what's the difference?**

A

한국어를 해요 translates to "I speak Korean" and focuses on the ability or skill to speak and understand Korean.

한국어로 해요 indicates that the language currently being spoken is Korean, rather than focusing on the speaker's proficiency. It translates to "I speak in Korean."

In short, **한국어를 해요** talks about the skill or ability to speak Korean, while **한국어로 해요** points to the fact that Korean is the language being spoken at the moment.

4. Purpose or Use — Translates as "for"

(으)로 is also used to indicate the purpose or use of a noun in a specific action. In this case, it functions similarly to the English word "for."

e.g. 아침으로 for breakfast

점심으로 for lunch

저녁으로 for dinner

선물로 for a gift

VOCAB
아침 morning, breakfast
점심 lunchtime, lunch
저녁 evening, dinner

When you use (으)로 in these contexts, you're specifying what something is being used for or the purpose of the action.

아침으로 샐러드를 먹었어요.

I had salad for breakfast.

점심으로 한국 음식을 먹었어요.

I had Korean food for lunch.

저녁으로 스테이크를 먹었어요.

I had steak for dinner.

친구 생일 선물로 목걸이를 샀어요.

I bought a necklace for my friend's birthday gift.

Quiz

▶ TRACK 32

1 True or False

① (으)로 and (이)랑 both mean "with," and they are interchangeable.

☐ / ☐
TRUE   FALSE

② When a noun ends with the consonant ㄹ and is combined with (으)로, it should be written as 로 (e.g., 연필로, 지하철로).

☐ / ☐
TRUE   FALSE

2 Fill in the blank with the correct word and particle.

① 제주도에 ☐☐☐☐☐ 갈 거예요.

I will go to Jeju island by plane.

② ☐☐☐☐☐ 썼어요.

I wrote it with my hand. (= I hand-wrote it.)

③ 현주 생일 ☐☐☐☐☐ 뭐 샀어?

What did you buy for the Hyeonju's birthday gift?

④ ☐☐☐☐☐ 뭐 먹었어요?

What did you have for breakfast?

3 Which one means "I speak Korean." in terms of proficiency?

① 한국어를 해요.

② 한국어로 해요.

ANSWER

1 ① F ② T

2 ① 비행기로 ② 손으로
  ③ 선물로 ④ 아침으로

3 ①

5. Choice

The last usage of (으)로 is indicating one's choice among options. When you're picking between different things, (으)로 helps mark the choice you go with.

e.g. **A** 이거랑 저거 중에서 뭐로 살 거예요?

Which one among this and that will you buy?

B 저거로 살 거예요.

I'll buy that one.

VOCAB

noun 중에서 among (used to indicate a selection from a group of nouns)

뭐 what (a question word; can sometimes be used to mean "which")

→ A and B both use the (으)로 particle to indicate the choice they're making among different options.

(으)로 is also commonly used when placing an order.

e.g. **A 뭐로 드릴까요?**

Which one shall I give you? (= What can I get you?)

B 라떼로 주세요.

Latte, please.

C 비빔밥으로 주세요.

Bibimbap, please.

In these examples, **(으)로** is used to show the specific choice or item you want when ordering something.

You might notice some of the verbs we haven't covered yet, like **드리다** and **주시다**. These are all honorific verbs of **주다**.
The word **주세요** means "please give me" and comes from **주시다**.
주세요 is often used when making requests in a polite way.

You can also simply say "Noun **주세요**" to ask for something.

e.g. **커피 주세요.**

Coffee, please.

차 주세요.

Tea, please.

1 Select the correct particle in the parentheses.

이거(로 / 에) 사요.

Let's get this one.

2 Imagine you're placing an order at a café. How would you politely request the following?

A 뭐로 드릴까요?

What can I get you?

B [   ].

Americano, please.

(Americano: 아메리카노)

ANSWER

1 로

2 아메리카노(로) 주세요

1   Select ALL the correct particles for the blank.

이번 주말에 언니 ☐ 놀 거예요.

I will hang out with my sister this weekend.

① 를   ② 랑   ③ 하고   ④ 와   ⑤ 로

2   Select the correct meaning of each particle in the sentence.

친구들하고 백화점에서 옷이랑 신발을 살 거예요. (옷: clothes, 신발: shoes)

① 하고 — (with / and)
② 이랑 — (with / and)

3   Select the correct particle in the parentheses.

공항(에 / 에서) 버스(로 / 랑) 갈 거예요.

I will go to the airport by bus.

4   Select one sentence where (으)로 is INCORRECTLY used, and fill in the
    blank with the correct particle.

① 아래로 내려갔어요. It went down.
② 비행기로 여행해요. I travel by plane.
③ 점심으로 빵을 먹었어요. I had bread for lunch.
④ 저는 한국어로 영어를 해요. I speak Korean and English.
⑤ 호텔에서 집으로 돌아갈 거예요. I will go back home from the hotel.

☐

5 Select the correct particle for the blank.

뭐 [ ] 샀어요?

Which one did you buy?

① 로   ② 랑   ③ 하고

6 Translate each sentence in the –요 ending 존댓말.

① I have a younger sister and a younger brother. (Use 여동생 and 남동생.)

_____

② I studied Korean at the library with my friend yesterday.

_____

③ I will buy shoes for mom's gift.

_____

④ **A** 뭐로 드릴까요?

    B This one, please.

_____

ANSWER

1 ②, ③, ④

2 ① with ② and

3 에, 로

4 ④ 로→랑, 하고 or 와

5 ①

6 ① 여동생이랑/하고/과 남동생이 있어요.

    ② 어제 친구랑/하고/와 도서관에서 한국어를 공부했어요.

    ③ 엄마 선물로 신발을 살 거예요.

    ④ 이거(로) 주세요.

CHAPTER 10

도 & 만
More Essential
Particles (2)

In this chapter, you will learn about the uses of the particles 도 and 만's usages and how they can be combined with other particles.

The form of 도 and 만 stay the same. They are not affected by what the noun ends with.

1 도 - too, also

Let's start with the example sentences.

e.g. 저는 한국 사람이에요. 지수도 한국 사람이에요.

I'm Korean. Jisu is also Korean.

저는 남동생이 있어요. 언니도 있어요.

I have a younger brother. I also have an older sister.

아침으로 빵을 먹었어요. 우유도 마셨어요.

I had bread for breakfast. I also had milk.

A 등산을 좋아해요. I like hiking.

B 저도요. Me too.

The particle 도 indicates that this noun, in addition to a previously mentioned noun, also applies in the same context.

도 cannot be used together with subject or object markers—it stands alone. Even if it's used by itself, the context makes it easy to understand whether the marked noun is the subject or object.

지수가도 한국사람이에요. (×)

→ 지수도 한국 사람이에요.

우유를도 마셨어요. (×)

→ 우유도 마셨어요.

However, except for the topic, subject, and object markers, **도** can be combined with other particles like **에**, **에서**, **(으)로**, or **에게/한테**.

In these combinations, the other particle always comes **before** **도**.

e.g. 한국에 친구가 있어요. <u>일본에도</u> 친구가 있어요.

일본도에(×)

I have a friend in Korea. I also have a friend in Japan.

학교에서 한국어를 배웠어요. <u>인터넷에서도</u> 배웠어요.

인터넷도에서 (×)

I learned Korean in school. I also learned it on the Internet.

친구한테 선물을 보냈어요. <u>부모님께도</u> 보냈어요.

부모님도께(×)

I sent a gift to my friend. I also sent one to my parents.

When **도** is followed by a negative verb, it corresponds to "either" in English.

e.g. **지금 지갑이 없어요. 가방도 없어요.**

I don't have my wallet right now. I don't have a bag either.

저는 요리를 못해요. 운동도 못해요.

I'm not good at cooking. Neither at sports.

지수 씨가 안[*] 왔어요. 민호 씨도 안 왔어요.

Jisu didn't come. Neither did Minho.

* **안** is a negation adverb that comes before a verb to add the meaning of "not."

Quiz

▶ **TRACK 34**

1 Fill in the blank with the correct particle.

한국을 좋아해요. 한국어 ▢ 배워요.

I like Korea. I also learn Korean.

2 Fill in the blank with the correct combination of particles.

아빠가 주말 ▢ 일해요.

My dad works on the weekends as well.

ANSWER

1 도   **2** 에도

2 만 - only

Let's start with some example sentences.

e.g. **커피에 설탕만 넣었어요.**

I only put sugar in the coffee.

하루 종일 드라마만 봤어요.

I only watched dramas all day.

제 친구들은 모두 형제가 있어요. 저만 없어요.

All of my friends have siblings. Only I don't have one.

VOCAB
하루종일 all day long
모두 all, everyone

Like **도**, **만** can mark subjects and objects without needing to use subject or object markers.

However, unlike **도**, it is acceptable to use **만** together with these markers.

e.g. **제 아내만을 사랑해요.**

I only love my wife.

가족 중에서 엄마만이 요리를 잘해요.

Among my family, only mom's good at cooking.

It's more common to use just **만** alone without the subject/object markers, but when you want to emphasize that it is *only* that particular noun, it's natural to use them together.

만 can also be combined with other particles, and in these combinations, the other particle comes **before** 만.

> e.g. **이번 여름에 집에만 있을 거예요.**
> I'm only going to stay at home this summer.
>
> **저는 학교에서만 공부해요.**
> I only study at school.
>
> **한국어를 책으로만 배웠어요.**
> I only learned Korean with a book.
>
> **이 기차는 서울역까지만 가요.**
> This train only goes as far as Seoul Station.

As an exception, when **으로** and **만** are combined, both **으로만** and **만으로** are correct.

> **책만으로** √
> **책으로만** √

Quiz
TRACK 35

1 Fill in the blank with the correct particle.

> **제 여동생은 소설책 ☐ 읽어요.**
> My younger sister only reads a novel.

2 Fill in the blank with the correct combination of particles.

> **저녁 ☐ 샤워를 해요.**
> I take a shower only at night.

EXERCISE

1   Fill in the blank with the correct particle.

① 저는 포도를 좋아해요. 딸기 [＿＿] 좋아해요.

   I like grapes. I also like strawberries.

② 아침으로 주스 [＿＿] 마셨어요.

   I only had juice for breakfast.

2   True or False

① 도 can be used together with subject and object markers.
   TRUE / FALSE

② 만 must always be used with subject and object markers.
   TRUE / FALSE

③ 도 and 만 come second in the combination when combined with other particles such as 에, 에서 or 까지.
   TRUE / FALSE

3   Fill in the blank with the correct combination of particles.

① A: 한국 사람들은 숟가락으로 밥을 먹어요.

   Koreans eat with spoons.

   B: 젓가락 [＿＿＿＿] 먹어요.

   They also eat with chopsticks.

② 지수랑 친해요. 하나 [＿＿＿＿] 친해요.

   I'm close with Jisu. I'm also close with Hana.

4 **Translate the following sentences in the –요 ending 존댓말.**

① My friends don't know Korean. Only I know.

_____

② I'm good at sports. I'm also good at driving.
[Use 운동(sports) and 운전(driving).]

_____

③ I only work at the office.
[Use 회사(office, company).]

_____

④ I don't have it either.

_____

⑤ I sent a gift only to my friend.

_____

⑥ I sent only a gift to my friend.

_____

ANSWER

1 ① 도 ② 만

2 ① F ② F ③ T

3 ① 으로도 ② 와도/랑도/하고도

4 ① 제 친구들은 한국어를 몰라요. 저만 알아요.
 ② 저는 운동을 잘해요. 운전도 잘해요.
 ③ 저는 회사에서만 일해요.
 ④ 저도 없어요.
 ⑤ 제 친구한테만/에게만 선물을 보냈어요.
 ⑥ 제 친구한테/에게 선물만 보냈어요.

CHAPTER 11

Adjectives

In this chapter, you'll learn two different ways to use
Korean adjectives in a sentence.

Adjectives are words that describe the emotions, characteristics, or a state of a person or thing.

For example, in these sentences,

선생님은 친절해요.

The teacher is kind.

이 신발은 커요.

These shoes are big.

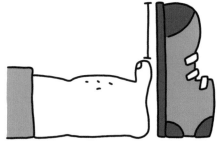

친절하다 (to be kind) and 크다 (to be big) are adjectives that describe the teacher's personality and the shoes' appearance, respectively.

As you can see from the examples, adjectives are placed at the end of a sentence and are conjugated, just like verbs. In fact, another term for adjectives is "descriptive verbs," which shows that adjectives can function similarly to verbs in sentences.

Other than this, adjectives can also come right before a noun to directly modify[*] it.

[*] To modify means to add information or specify details about another word. Adjectives can only modify nouns.

For example, you can say,

친절한 사람을 만났어요.

I met a <u>kind</u> person.

큰 신발을 샀어요.

I bought <u>big</u> shoes.

In each sentence, 친절한 (kind) and 큰 (big) are giving direct information about the nouns that follow, 사람 (person) and 신발 (shoes).

In Korean grammar, these are called the **modifier form** of adjectives.

As you can see, the conjugated form of an adjective is different from its modifier form.

Both forms of adjectives are commonly used, so it would be helpful to learn how to use each one.

We'll begin by learning the conjugation rules for adjectives.

Adjective's Conjugation

1

The conjugation rules for adjectives follow <u>the same rules</u> as verbs.

1. Regular Rules

 연습

If you remember the conjugation rules from the chapter on verbs, you'll be able to easily conjugate the adjectives below.

	Present Tense	Past Tense	Future Tense
좋다 (to be good)			
많다 (to be many [in quantity])			
적다 (to be few, little [in quantity])			
작다 (to be small [in size])			
길다 (to be long)			
짧다 (to be short)			
싸다 (to be cheap)			
비싸다 (to be expensive)			
느리다 (to be slow)			
행복하다 (to be happy)			
건강하다 (to be healthy)			
친절하다 (to be kind)			
맛있다 (to be delicious)			
재미있다 (to be fun)			

	Present Tense	Past Tense	Future Tense
좋다 (to be good)	좋아(요)	좋았어(요)	좋을 거야/거예요
많다 (to be many [in quantity])	많아(요)	많았어(요)	많을 거야/거예요
적다 (to be few, little [in quantity])	적어(요)	적었어(요)	적을 거야/거예요
작다 (to be small [in size])	작아(요)	작았어(요)	작을 거야/거예요
길다 (to be long)	길어(요)	길었어(요)	길 거야/거예요
짧다 (to be short)	짧아(요)	짧았어(요)	짧을 거야/거예요
싸다 (to be cheap)	싸(요)	쌌어(요)	쌀 거야/거예요
비싸다 (to be expensive)	비싸(요)	비쌌어(요)	비쌀 거야/거예요
느리다 (to be slow)	느려(요)	느렸어(요)	느릴 거야/거예요
행복하다 (to be happy)	행복해(요)	행복했어(요)	행복할 거야/거예요
건강하다 (to be healthy)	건강해(요)	건강했어(요)	건강할 거야/거예요
친절하다 (to be kind)	친절해(요)	친절했어(요)	친절할 거야/거예요
맛있다 (to be delicious)	맛있어(요)	맛있었어(요)	맛있을 거야/거예요
재미있다 (to be fun)	재미있어(요)	재미있었어(요)	재미있을 거야/거예요

Quiz

▶ TRACK 36

Fill in the blank with the correctly conjugated adjective.

1 이 고양이는 [   ]요.

This cat is <u>small</u>.

2 사람이 [   ]요.

There are <u>many</u> people.

3 어제 날씨가 [　　　]요.

The weather <u>was good</u> yesterday.

4 제 머리는 [　　　]요.

My hair <u>is long.</u>

5 기차가 너무 [　　　]요.

The train <u>is too slow.</u>

6 저는 [　　　]요.

<u>I am healthy.</u>

7 한국어 공부가 [　　　　]요.

Studying Korean <u>will be fun.</u>

ANSWER

1 작아   **2** 많아   **3** 좋았어   **4** 길어

5 느려   **6** 건강해   **7** 재미있을 거예

---

2. Irregular Rules

Just like verbs, some adjectives in Korean follow irregular conjugation rules.

Many stem forms that are irregular in verbs are typically irregular in adjectives as well.

In this chapter, we'll focus on the most common irregular adjectives and their unique conjugation patterns.

(1) Adjectives that end with ㅂ

There are many Korean adjectives with stems that end in the final consonant ㅂ, and these follow irregular conjugation rules. They each follow different irregular patterns when conjugated into the present (& past) and future tense.

Let's first learn the rules for present and past tense.

❶ Present & Past Tense Conjugation

> **Present Tense : Remove ㅂ from the stem and add 워**

> **Past Tense : Present Tense + ㅆ + 어**

	Present	Past
덥다 (to be hot - weather) →	더워(요)	더웠어(요)
춥다 (to be cold - weather) →	추워(요)	추웠어(요)
뜨겁다 (to be hot - touch) →	뜨거워(요)	뜨거웠어(요)
차갑다 (to be cold - touch) →	차가워(요)	차가웠어(요)

 연습

With this rule, now you can try conjugating each adjective below, in present and past tense.

	Present Tense	Past Tense
맵다 (to be spicy)		
아름답다 (to be beautiful)		
귀엽다 (to be cute)		
쉽다 (to be easy)		
어렵다 (to be hard, difficult)		
가깝다 (to be close)		

ANSWER

	Present Tense	Past Tense		Present Tense	Past Tense
맵다	매워(요)	매웠어(요)	쉽다	쉬워(요)	쉬웠어(요)
아름답다	아름다워(요)	아름다웠어(요)	어렵다	어려워(요)	어려웠어(요)
귀엽다	귀여워(요)	귀여웠어(요)	가깝다	가까워(요)	가까웠어(요)

덥다 vs. 뜨겁다 (to be hot)

춥다 vs. 차갑다 (to be cold)

Both 덥다 and 뜨겁다 mean "to be hot," and both 춥다 and 차갑다 mean "to be cold." So, what's the difference?

덥다 and 춥다 are used to describe the weather—either the weather itself or the physical sensation you feel in it.

> e.g. **여름은 날씨가 더워요.** The weather is hot in summer.
>
> **겨울은 날씨가 추워요.** The weather is cold in winter.

On the other hand, 뜨겁다 and 차갑다 are used when you touch something (or something touches you) and feel that it's hot or cold. These words can also be used in a figurative sense, like "hot reactions (enthusiastic reactions)" or "cold personality."

> e.g. **햇빛이 너무 뜨거워요.**
>
> The sunlight is too hot. (= The sun is too strong.)

물이 차가워요.

The water is cold.

사람들의 반응이 뜨거웠어요.

The people's reactions were enthusiastic.

지수는 성격이 차가워요.

Jisu has a cold personality.

Quiz

▶ TRACK 37

Fill in the blank with the correctly conjugated adjectives.

1 날씨가 너무 [   ].

The weather is too hot.

2 어제 너무 [   ].

It was too cold yesterday.

3 커피가 너무 [   ].

The coffee is too hot.

4 음식이 너무 [   ].

The food was too spicy.

5 아기가 [   ].

The baby is cute.

6 울산은 부산하고* [   ].

Ulsan is close to Busan.

* In Korean, we say something is close "with" something else when talking about location closeness, rather than close "to." This is why 하고 is used in this sentence.

ANSWER

1 더워요   2 추웠어요   3 뜨거워요
4 매웠어요   5 귀여워요   6 가까워요

❷ Future Tense

> **Remove ㅂ from the stem and add 울 + 거이다**

덥다 ⟶ 더울 거야/거예요 (will be hot)

춥다 ⟶ 추울 거야/거예요 (will be cold)

 연습

By following this rule, you can fill in the blank below to complete the future tense conjugation.

① 뜨겁다 → [   ] 거야/거예요 (will be hot)

② 차갑다 → [   ] 거야/거예요 (will be cold)

③ 맵다 → [   ] 거야/거예요 (will be spicy)

④ 아름답다 → [   ] 거야/거예요 (will be beautiful)

⑤ 귀엽다 → [   ] 거야/거예요 (will be cute)

⑥ 쉽다 → [   ] 거야/거예요 (will be easy)

⑦ 어렵다 → [   ] 거야/거예요 (will be difficult)

⑧ 가깝다 → [   ] 거야/거예요 (will be close)

ANSWER
① 뜨거울   ② 차가울   ③ 매울   ④ 아름다울
⑤ 귀여울   ⑥ 쉬울   ⑦ 어려울   ⑧ 가까울

Quiz

Fill in the blank with the correctly conjugated adjectives.

1　내일 날씨가 [　　　　] 거예요.

The weather <u>will be cold</u> tomorrow.

2　국물이 [　　　　] 거예요.

The broth <u>will be hot</u>.

3　[　　　　] 거예요. 물을 더 넣어요.

It <u>will be spicy</u>. Put more water in it.

4　가을 풍경이 매우 [　　　　] 거예요.

The autumn view <u>will be</u> so <u>beautiful</u>.

5　[　　　　] 거예요. 제가 도와줄게요.

It <u>will be hard</u>. I'll help you.

ANSWER

1 추울　2 뜨거울　3 매울

4 아름다울　5 어려울

Q The verbs 입다 (to wear) and 잡다 (to catch) both end in ㅂ but conjugate regularly as 입어 and 잡아. Is this because the conjugation rule is different for verbs and adjectives?

A

No, it's not different for verbs and adjectives. 입다 and 잡다 are simply exceptions to the ㅂ-irregular rule and follow regular conjugation instead. There are verbs where the ㅂ-irregular rule *does* apply, and there are adjectives where it *does not* apply.

For example:

> 눕다 (to lie down [verb]) → **누워, 누웠어, 누울 거예요** (irregular)
>
> 좁다 (to be narrow [adjective]) → **좁아, 좁았어, 좁을 거예요** (regular)

It's true that there are more adjectives follow the ㅂ-irregular rule compared to verbs. However, it ultimately depends on each word rather than being strictly different for verbs and adjectives.

Similar to this, there are verbs ending with ㄷ that follow either the regular or irregular conjugation rule. For example, you may have noticed that both 닫다 (to close) and 듣다 (to listen) end with ㄷ, but 닫다 follows the regular conjugation rule, whereas 듣다 follows an irregular rule.

These kinds of "exceptions within irregular rules" aren't very common, so don't worry too much. Simply focus on getting familiar with the final conjugated form of each word.

(2) Adjectives that end with ㄹ

We already learned the conjugation rules for ㄹ-ending verbs and that their irregularity only appears in the future tense. The same rule applies to adjectives.

길다 (to be long) ⟶ 길 거야/거예요

As you can see with **길다**, instead of adding **을** to the stem and saying **길을 거예요** (x), you just use the stem itself to say **길 거야** or **길 거예요** (will be long).

연습

Complete the future tense conjugation below.

① **멀다** (to be far) → [   ] 거야/거예요

② **달다** (to be sweet) → [   ] 거야/거예요

ANSWER
① 멀 ② 달

Quiz

▶ TRACK 39

Fill in the blank with the correctly conjugated adjective.

우리 집에서 우체국까지 조금 [   ]요.

From my house to the post office, it will be a bit far.

ANSWER
멀 거예

(3) Adjectives that end with —

For verbs or adjectives ending in —, the future tense follows the regular rule, and it's only the present and past tense that follow irregular patterns.

As we've already learned, the past tense is formed by simply adding the final consonant **ㅆ** to the present tense stem, followed by **어**.

So for this irregular rule, I'll just focus on explaining the present tense conjugation.

For verbs or adjectives that end with —, there are two different conjugation rules.

Sometimes, the — is replaced with ㅏ, and other times it is replaced with ㅓ.

❶ Replace ― with ㅏ

If the syllable before ― in the stem contains ㅏ or ㅗ, the ― is replaced with ㅏ.

바쁘다, 아프다, 고프다, 나쁘다

For these adjectives, the character right before the ― vowel has either ㅏ or ㅗ.

In these cases, the ― is replaced with ㅏ when conjugated.

바쁘다 (to be busy) ⟶ 바빠

아프다 (to be sick) ⟶ 아파

(배가) 고프다 (to be hungry) ⟶ 고파

나쁘다 (to be bad) ⟶ 나빠

❷ Replace ― with ㅓ

If the stem has only one syllable with ― (e.g., 크다 or 쓰다), or when the syllable before ― has a vowel other than ㅏ or ㅓ, the ― is replaced with ㅓ.

One-syllable stem with ― vowel : 크다, 쓰다

Two-syllable stem where the vowel before ― is not ㅏ or ㅗ : 예쁘다, 슬프다

크다 (to be big) ⟶ 커

쓰다 (to be bitter) ⟶ 써

예쁘다 (to be pretty) ⟶ 예뻐

슬프다 (to be sad) ⟶ 슬퍼

쓰다 as a verb means "to write" or "to use," and as an adjective, it means "to be bitter." Despite the difference in meaning, the conjugation rules are the same for both.

Q In the chapter on verbs, we've learned that 모르다 is conjugated as 몰라, instead of 모라.
Why does it follow a different rule if it ends with ―?

A

Even though 모르다 ends with ―, it's classified as a 르-ending verb, not just a simple ― ending verb. 르-ending verbs (such as 모르다, 마르다, 부르다, etc.), follow a different conjugation pattern from other ― ending verbs. We will learn this rule in more detail in *Korean Grammar Palette for Beginners 2*.

Quiz

▶ TRACK 40

Fill in the blank with the correctly conjugated adjectives.

1 저 요즘 [   ]요.
   I am busy these days.

2 어제 [   ]요.
   I was sick yesterday.

3 디자인이 정말 [   ]요.
   The design is really pretty.

4 바지가 저한테 너무 [   ]요.
   These pants are too big for me.

5 배가 [   ]요.
   I am hungry.

6 지수 씨가 떠나면 [   ]요.
   If Jisu leaves, I will be sad.

ANSWER
1 바빠
2 아팠어
3 예뻐
4 커
5 고파
6 슬플 거예

Adjective's Modifier Form

Just like with conjugation, the modifier form has both regular and irregular rules.

If a word follows the regular rule in conjugation, it usually follows the regular rule in the modifier form.

Likewise, if it follows an irregular rule in conjugation, the modifier form will usually follow the irregular rule as well.

There are some exceptions, of course. For example, adjectives that end with — follow an irregular rule in conjugation, but when converting to the modifier form, they follow the regular rule.

First, let's learn about the regular rule, and then we'll explore the common irregular rules.

1. Regular Rules

Turning adjectives into their modifier form is very simple.

$$\boxed{\text{stem}} \ + \ \boxed{\text{ㄴ/은}}$$

If the stem ends with a vowel, you add the final consonant ㄴ, and if it ends with a consonant, you add 은.

For example:

크다 (to be big) ⟶ 큰 (big)

작다 (to be small) ⟶ 작은 (small)

연습

Now, you can convert the adjectives below into their modifier forms.

좋다 (to be good)	
많다 (to be many [in quantity])	
적다 (to be few, little [in quantity])	
작다 (to be small [in size])	
짧다 (to be short)	
싸다 (to be cheap)	
비싸다 (to be expensive)	
느리다 (to be slow)	
행복하다 (to be happy)	
건강하다 (to be healthy)	
친절하다 (to be kind)	
바쁘다 (to be busy)	
아프다 (to be sick)	
배가 고프다 (to be hungry)	
나쁘다 (to be bad)	
크다 (to be big)	
쓰다 (to be bitter)	
예쁘다 (to be pretty)	
슬프다 (to be sad)	

ANSWER

좋다	→	좋은		많다	→	많은
적다	→	적은		작다	→	작은
짧다	→	짧은		싸다	→	싼
비싸다	→	비싼		느리다	→	느린
행복하다	→	행복한		건강하다	→	건강한
친절하다	→	친절한		바쁘다	→	바쁜
아프다	→	아픈		배가 고프다	→	배가 고픈
나쁘다	→	나쁜		크다	→	큰
쓰다	→	쓴		예쁘다	→	예쁜
슬프다	→	슬픈				

Quiz

Fill in the blank with the correct modifier forms of adjectives.

1 [_____] 친구가 있어요.

I have a <u>good</u> friend.

2 [_____] 고양이를 봤어요.

I saw a <u>small</u> cat.

3 엄마가 [_____] 가방을 샀어요.

Mom bought an <u>expensive</u> bag.

4 [_____] 가족이랑 같이 살고 있어요.

I live together with a <u>happy</u> family.

5 [_____] 머리가 예뻐요.

The <u>short</u> hair is pretty.

6 병원에 [_____] 환자들이 있어요.

There are <u>sick</u> patients in the hospital.

7 [_____] 커피를 좋아해요.

I like <u>bitter</u> coffee.

8 여자 친구한테 [_____] 꽃을 선물로 줬어요.

I gave <u>pretty</u> flowers as a gift to my girlfriend.

ANSWER

1 좋은 2 작은 3 비싼 4 행복한
5 짧은 6 아픈 7 쓴 8 예쁜

(1) Adjectives that end with ㅂ

> **Remove ㅂ and add 운**

덥다 (to be hot) ⟶ 더운 (hot)

춥다 (to be cold) ⟶ 추운 (cold)

 연습

Now, you can convert the adjectives below into their modifier forms.

뜨겁다 (to be hot)	
차갑다 (to be cold)	
맵다 (to be spicy)	
아름답다 (to be beautiful)	
귀엽다 (to be cute)	
쉽다 (to be easy)	
어렵다 (to be difficult)	
가깝다 (to be close)	

ANSWER

뜨겁다	→	뜨거운
차갑다	→	차가운
맵다	→	매운
아름답다	→	아름다운
귀엽다	→	귀여운
쉽다	→	쉬운
어렵다	→	어려운
가깝다	→	가까운

(2) Adjectives that end with ㄹ

> **Replace ㄹ with ㄴ**

길다 (to be long) ⟶ 긴 (long)

달다 (to be sweet) ⟶ 단 (sweet)

멀다 (to be far) ⟶ 먼 (far)

(3) Adjectives that end with 있다 and 없다

Do you remember the adjectives **맛있다** (to be delicious) and **재미있다** (to be fun)?

Their modifier forms are **맛있는** and **재미있는**.

> *e.g.* 맛있는 음식을 먹었어요.
>
> 재미있는 영화를 봐요.

As you can see, **는** is added to the stem, instead of **은**.

All words that include **있다** and **없다** are like this.

맛없다 (to be tasteless, taste bad) ⟶ 맛없는 (tasteless)

재미없다 (to be boring) ⟶ 재미없는 (boring)

> *e.g.* 맛없는 커피를 마셨어요.
>
> 재미없는 책을 읽었어요.

Quiz

Fill in the blank with the correct modifier forms of adjectives.

1　[   ] 물을 마셨어요.
I drank hot water.

2　[   ] 물로 샤워했어요.
I had a shower with cold water.

3　[   ] 날씨를 안 좋아해요.
I don't like hot weather.

4　[   ] 이야기예요.
It's a beautiful story.

5　[   ] 음식을 자주 먹어요.
I often eat spicy food.

6　기차역이 [   ] 거리에 있어요.
The train station is at a close distance.

7　우리는 [   ] 다리를 건넜어요.
We crossed a long bridge.

8　[   ] 음식을 많이 먹었어요.
I ate a lot of delicious food.

ANSWER
1 뜨거운　2 차가운　3 더운
4 아름다운　5 매운　6 가까운
7 긴　8 맛있는

연습

Fill in the table with the present, past, and future tense conjugations,
as well as the modifier forms for each adjective.

	Present Tense	Past Tense	Future Tense	Modifier
좋다 (to be good)				
나쁘다 (to be bad)				
크다 (to be big)				
작다 (to be small)				
많다 (to be many)				
적다 (to be few)				
길다 (to be long)				
짧다 (to be short)				
싸다 (to be cheap)				
비싸다 (to be expensive)				
행복하다 (to be happy)				
슬프다 (to be sad)				
건강하다 (to be healthy)				
아프다 (to be sick)				
덥다 (to be hot[weather])				
춥다 (to be cold[weather])				
뜨겁다 (to be hot[touch])				
차갑다 (to be cold[touch])				
아름답다 (to be beautiful)				
예쁘다 (to be pretty)				
귀엽다 (to be cute)				
쓰다 (to be bitter)				
달다 (to be sweet)				
맵다 (to be spicy)				

	Present Tense	Past Tense	Future Tense	Modifier
쉽다 (to be easy)				
어렵다 (to be difficult)				
가깝다 (to be close)				
멀다 (to be far)				
느리다 (to be slow)				
친절하다 (to be kind)				
바쁘다 (to be busy)				
배가 고프다 (to be hungry)				
맛있다 (to be delicious)				
맛없다 (to taste bad)				
재미있다 (to be fun)				
재미없다 (to be boring)				

▶ TRACK 43

ANSWER

	Present Tense	Past Tense	Future Tense	Modifier
좋다 (to be good)	좋아(요)	좋았어(요)	좋을 거야/거예요	좋은
나쁘다 (to be bad)	나빠(요)	나빴어(요)	나쁠 거야/거예요	나쁜
크다 (to be big)	커(요)	컸어(요)	클 거야/거예요	큰
작다 (to be small)	작아(요)	작았어(요)	작을 거야/거예요	작은
많다 (to be many)	많아(요)	많았어(요)	많을 거야/거예요	많은
적다 (to be few)	적어(요)	적었어(요)	적을 거야/거예요	적은
길다 (to be long)	길어(요)	길었어(요)	길 거야/거예요	긴
짧다 (to be short)	짧아(요)	짧았어(요)	짧을 거야/거예요	짧은
싸다 (to be cheap)	싸(요)	쌌어(요)	쌀 거야/거예요	싼
비싸다 (to be expensive)	비싸(요)	비쌌어(요)	비쌀 거야/거예요	비싼
행복하다 (to be happy)	행복해(요)	행복했어(요)	행복할 거야/거예요	행복한

	Present Tense	Past Tense	Future Tense	Modifier
슬프다 (to be sad)	슬퍼(요)	슬펐어(요)	슬플 거야/거예요	슬픈
건강하다 (to be healthy)	건강해(요)	건강했어(요)	건강할 거야/거예요	건강한
아프다 (to be sick)	아파(요)	아팠어(요)	아플 거야/거예요	아픈
덥다 (to be hot[weather])	더워(요)	더웠어(요)	더울 거야/거예요	더운
춥다 (to be cold[weather])	추워(요)	추웠어(요)	추울 거야/거예요	추운
뜨겁다 (to be hot[touch])	뜨거워(요)	뜨거웠어(요)	뜨거울 거야/거예요	뜨거운
차갑다 (to be cold[touch])	차가워(요)	차가웠어(요)	차가울 거야/거예요	차가운
아름답다 (to be beautiful)	아름다워(요)	아름다웠어(요)	아름다울 거야/거예요	아름다운
예쁘다 (to be pretty)	예뻐(요)	예뻤어(요)	예쁠 거야/거예요	예쁜
귀엽다 (to be cute)	귀여워(요)	귀여웠어(요)	귀여울 거야/거예요	귀여운
쓰다 (to be bitter)	써(요)	썼어(요)	쓸 거야/거예요	쓴
달다 (to be sweet)	달아(요)	달았어(요)	달 거야/거예요	단
맵다 (to be spicy)	매워(요)	매웠어(요)	매울 거야/거예요	매운
쉽다 (to be easy)	쉬워(요)	쉬웠어(요)	쉬울 거야/거예요	쉬운
어렵다 (to be difficult)	어려워(요)	어려웠어(요)	어려울 거야/거예요	어려운
가깝다 (to be close)	가까워(요)	가까웠어(요)	가까울 거야/거예요	가까운
멀다 (to be far)	멀어(요)	멀었어(요)	멀 거야/거예요	먼
느리다 (to be slow)	느려(요)	느렸어(요)	느릴 거야/거예요	느린
친절하다 (to be kind)	친절해(요)	친절했어(요)	친절할 거야/거예요	친절한
바쁘다 (to be busy)	바빠(요)	바빴어(요)	바쁠 거야/거예요	바쁜
배가 고프다 (to be hungry)	배가 고파(요)	배가 고팠어(요)	배가 고플 거야/거예요	배가 고픈
맛있다 (to be delicious)	맛있어(요)	맛있었어(요)	맛있을 거야/거예요	맛있는
맛없다 (to taste bad)	맛없어(요)	맛없었어(요)	맛없을 거야/거예요	맛없는
재미있다 (to be fun)	재미있어(요)	재미있었어(요)	재미있을 거야/거예요	재미있는
재미없다 (to be boring)	재미없어(요)	재미없었어(요)	재미없을 거야/거예요	재미없는

1 True or False

① Adjectives have both a conjugation form and
a modifier form.

☐ / ☐
TRUE   FALSE

② Adjectives follow completely different conjugation
rules from verbs.

☐ / ☐
TRUE   FALSE

③ In the sentence 좋은 책이에요, 좋은 is the
modifier form of an adjective.

☐ / ☐
TRUE   FALSE

2 Fill in the blank with the correct conjugated forms and modifier forms of each adjective.

	Present Tense	Modifier
① 넓다 (to be wide)		
② 시다 (to be sour)		
③ 밝다 (to be bright)		
④ 어둡다 (to be dark)		
⑤ 똑똑하다 (to be smart)		
⑥ 기쁘다 (to be happy, pleased)		

3 Fill in the blank with the most appropriate adjective from the box.

덥다   춥다   뜨겁다   차갑다

① A: 한국 날씨가 어때요? How's the weather in Korea?

B: 여름에는 ☐ 요. 겨울에는 ☐ 요.

② 앗, _____ !

아이고, _____ !

4   Look at the picture and fill in the blank with the appropriately conjugated adjective.

달다   맵다   많다   고프다   슬프다

① 공항에 사람이 [   ]요.

② 배가 [   ]요.

③ 영화가 [   ]요.

④ 라면이 [   ]요.

⑤ 과일이 [   ]요.

5 Select the sentence with the INCORRECT modifier form of an adjective and write the corrected form.

① 한국에서 친절한 사람을 만났어요.

② 부모님께 길은 편지를 보냈어요.

③ 슬픈 영화를 봤어요.

④ 카페에서 맛있는 커피를 마셨어요.

⑤ 가까운 편의점에 갔어요.

6 Select the sentence with the INCORRECT future tense adjective conjugation and correct it.

① 학교에서 집까지 가까울 거예요.

② 커피에 설탕을 많이 넣었어요. 달 거예요.

③ 배가 고플 거예요. 이거 먹어요.

④ 한국은 여름에 너무 덥을 거예요.

⑤ 그 영화가 재미있을 거예요.

7 Translate the following sentences in the −요 ending 존댓말. (All sentences, except for number 5, can have the subject omitted, assuming it is clear from the context.)

① You'll be hungry. Eat this.

_____

② I will read a fun book.

_____

③ It was a happy day. (하루: a day)

_____

④ I live in a small house.

_____

⑤ Korean is easy. (Use the particle 은/는)

_____

⑥ I bought a cheap bag. It's pretty. (가방: a bag)

_____

ANSWER

1   ① T   ② F   ③ T

2 | | Present Tense | Modifier |
| --- | --- | --- |
| ① 넓다 (to be wide) | 넓어 | 넓은 |
| ② 시다 (to be sour) | 셔 | 신 |
| ③ 밝다 (to be bright) | 밝아 | 밝은 |
| ④ 어둡다 (to be dark) | 어두워 | 어두운 |
| ⑤ 똑똑하다 (to be smart) | 똑똑해 | 똑똑한 |
| ⑥ 기쁘다 (to be happy, pleased) | 기뻐 | 기쁜 |

3   ① 더워, 추워   ② 뜨거워, 차가워
  * when talking to oneself, we usually use 반말.

4   ① 많아   ② 고파   ③ 슬퍼   ④ 매워   ⑤ 달아

5   ② 길은 → 긴
  ① I met a kind person in Korea.   ② I sent a long letter to my parents.
  ③ I watched a sad movie.   ④ I drank a delicious coffee at a café.
  ⑤ I went to a convenience store nearby.

6   ④ 덥을 → 더울
  ① It will be close from school to home.
  ② I put a lot of sugar in the coffee. It will be sweet.
  ③ You'll be hungry. Eat this.   ④ The summer will be too hot in Korea.
  ⑤ That movie will be fun.

7   ① 배가 고플 거예요. 이거 먹어요.   ② 재미있는 책을 읽을 거예요.
  ③ 행복한 하루였어요.   ④ 작은 집에 (or 집에서) 살아요.
  ⑤ 한국어는 쉬워요.   ⑥ 싼 가방을 샀어요. 예뻐요.

How to Say "This, Last, and Next" for Time References

How would you express phrases like "this week," "last month," or "next year" in Korean?

Here's the most common way, using mostly native Korean words:

This : 이번 (literally, this time)

Last : 저번 (literally, that time)

　　　지난 (literally, passed)

Next : 다음

+ **units of time**

　　Week: 주
　　Weekend: 주말
　　Month: 달

For example, "this week" is **이번 주**, "last month" is **저번/지난 달**, and "next weekend" is **다음 주말**.

> *e.g.* 이번 주에 **여행 갈 거예요**.
> I will go traveling this week.
>
> 저번 달에 **한국어 공부를 시작했어요**.
> I started studying Korean last month.
>
> 다음 주말에 **친척들을 만날 거예요**.
> I will meet my relatives next weekend.

As you can see from the examples, they are used with the time marker **에** since they are time nouns.

Then, how would you say "year"?

해 and **년** both mean "year," but **해** is a native Korean word, while **년** is a Sino-Korean word.

When talking about years, it's more natural and common to use the following words:

- this year: **올해** (native Korean)
- last year: **작년** (Sino-Korean)
- next year: **내년** (Sino-Korean)

While combinations like **이번 해**, **저번/지난 해**, or **다음 해** are still used, they are less common in everyday conversations.

년 is also used when writing out years.

2000년: the year 2000

2025년: the year 2025

 In a Nutshell

This Week	이번 주
Last Week	저번/지난 주
Next Week	다음 주
This/Last/Next Weekend	이번/저번/다음 주말
This Month	이번 달
Last Month	저번/지난 달
Next Month	다음 달
This Year	올해
Last Year	작년
Next Year	내년

CHAPTER 12

안, -지 않다
Negating Verbs
and Adjectives

In this chapter, you will learn how to express negation
for verbs and adjectives to say things like
"I don't like it" or "It's not good."

In Korean, there are two ways to use negative verbs and adjectives:

① 안 + verb/adjective conjugation

— Add the negative adverb 안 before the verb or adjective.

② verb/adjective-지 않다 $\xrightarrow{\text{and then}}$ conjugate 않다

— Add the negative verb ending -지 않다 to the verb or adjective stem, and then 않다 is conjugated according to the tense.

Let's start by practicing how to make negative sentences using 안.

1 안

The example sentences below will help you easily understand how to use it.

❶ Present Tense

e.g. **아침을 안 먹어요.**

I don't have breakfast.

커피가 안 뜨거워요.

The coffee isn't hot.

❷ Past Tense

e.g. **아침을 안 먹었어요.**

I didn't have breakfast.

커피가 안 뜨거웠어요.

The coffee wasn't hot.

❸ Future Tense

e.g. **아침을 안 먹을 거예요.**

I will not have breakfast.

커피가 안 뜨거울 거예요.

The coffee won't be hot.

연습

Now, you can write the following negative sentences in Korean with **안**.

① [   ]   I don't live in Korea.

② [   ]   I don't like spicy food.

③ [   ]   It's not spicy.

④ [   ]   I didn't drink coffee today.

⑤ [   ]   I didn't read the letter.

⑥ [   ]   The shoes aren't pretty.

⑦ [   ]   Mom will not come home today.

⑧ [   ]   I won't go to school tomorrow.

⑨ [   ]   It won't be cold next week.

ANSWER

① 한국에 안 살아요.

② 매운 음식을 안 좋아해요.

③ 안 매워요.

④ 오늘 커피를 안 마셨어요.

⑤ 편지를 안 읽었어요.

⑥ 신발이 안 예뻐요.

⑦ 엄마는 오늘 집에 안 올 거예요.

⑧ 내일 학교에 안 갈 거예요.

⑨ 다음 주에 안 추울 거예요.

2 −지 않다

−지 않다 is a verb ending that comes after the stem of a verb or an adjective to express negatives.

The word **않다** is a verb, so it needs to be conjugated like any other verb, following the regular conjugation rules.

❶ Present Tense: V/A−지 않아요

e.g. **단 음식을 좋아하지 않아요.** = **단 음식을 안 좋아해요.**
I don't like sweet food.

제 머리가 길지 않아요. = **제 머리가 안 길어요.**
My hair isn't long.

❷ Past Tense: V/A−지 않았어요

e.g. **그 단어를 배우지 않았어요.** = **그 단어를 안 배웠어요.**
I didn't learn that word.

책이 비싸지 않았어요. = **책이 안 비쌌어요.**
The book wasn't expensive.

❸ Future Tense: V/A−지 않을 거예요

e.g. **양말을 신지 않을 거예요.** = **양말을 안 신을 거예요.**
I won't wear socks.

어렵지 않을 거예요. = **안 어려울 거예요.**
It won't be hard.

Now, you can use –지 않다 to write the following negative sentences in the –요 ending 존댓말.

① [   ] (채소: vegetable, 고기: meat)
My friend doesn't eat vegetables. He only eats meat.

② [   ]
The house isn't big. It's small.

③ [   ] (졸리다: to be sleepy)
I didn't drink coffee. I'm sleepy.

④ [   ] (웃기다: to be funny)
The movie wasn't sad. It was funny.

⑤ [   ]
I will not use English. I will only use Korean.

⑥ [   ]
There won't be many people.

ANSWER

① 제 친구는 채소를 먹지 않아요. 고기만 먹어요.

② 집이 크지 않아요. 작아요.

③ 커피를 마시지 않았어요. 졸려요.

④ 영화가 슬프지 않았어요. 웃겼어요.

⑤ 영어를 쓰지 않을 거예요. 한국어만 쓸 거예요.

⑥ 사람이 많지 않을 거예요.

3 Special Rule for Negating "Noun + 하다" Verbs

In the verb chapter, we learned that many verbs ending in **–하다** are made by combining a noun and the verb **하다** (to do).

For example, words like **공부하다** (to study), **생각하다** (to think), **운동하다** (to exercise), and **일하다** (to work) are created by combining the nouns **공부** (study), **생각** (thought), **운동** (exercise) and **일** (work) with **하다**.

When making negations with these verbs, there's a different rule, but **this rule only applies to 안** and does not apply to **–지 않다**.

You can make negations with **–지 않다** for these verbs the same way you would with other verbs.

 저는 집에서 일하지 않아요.
I don't work **at home.**

도서관에서 공부하지 않았어요.
I didn't study **at the library.**

운동하지 않을 거예요.
I won't exercise.

However, when using **안**, a slightly different rule applies.

Let's first take a look at some example sentences. Try to figure out the pattern on your own.

don't study	√ 공부 안 해요	x 안 공부해요
don't think	√ 생각 안 해요	x 안 생각해요
didn't exercise	√ 운동 안 했어요	x 안 운동했어요
won't work	√ 일 안 할 거예요	x 안 일할 거예요

Did you notice it?

Unlike other verbs, you don't put **안** in front of the full verb.

Instead, you separate the noun from **하다** and put **안** between them.

One more useful thing to know is that when a noun and **하다** are separated, the noun becomes the direct object of **하다**. So, you can add the object marker **을/를** to the separated noun.

> *e.g.* 공부 안 해요 = 공부를 안 해요
>
> 생각 안 해요 = 생각을 안 해요
>
> 운동 안 했어요 = 운동을 안 했어요
>
> 일 안 할 거예요 = 일을 안 할 거예요

It's pretty simple, right?

However when learning this rule, it can cause a few misunderstandings among students. Let's take a look at them so that you can avoid making these mistakes.

❶ This does NOT apply to <u>adjectives</u> with Noun+하다 form.

Aside from verbs, we've learned a lot of adjectives that end in **–하다**, haven't we?

For example, **건강하다** (to be healthy), **행복하다** (to be happy), and **친절하다** (to be kind) are all adjectives made by combining the nouns **건강** (health), **행복** (happiness), and **친절** (kindness) with **하다**.

When negating these adjectives with **안**, they don't follow the same rule as **–하다** ending verbs.

You can simply negate them like you would with any other adjectives.

> *e.g.* √ 안 건강하다   x 건강 안 하다
>
> √ 안 행복하다   x 행복 안 하다
>
> √ 안 친절하다   x 친절 안 하다

❷ Not all –하다 ending verbs are combinations of a noun and 하다.

For verbs like **좋아하다** (to like), **싫어하다** (to hate) and **정하다**(to decide), which do end in **–하다** but are not a combination of a noun and **하다**, you cannot separate **좋아** and **하다**, **싫어** and **하다**, or **정** and **하다**.

This means that you cannot negate them by putting **안** between them.

You can just say **안 좋아하다** (to not like), **안 싫어하다** (to not hate) or **안 정하다** (to not decide), instead of **좋아 안 하다**, **싫어 안 하다** or **정 안 하다**.

Quiz

▶ TRACK 46

Select the correct negation forms in the parentheses.

1 (운동 안 해 / 운동하지 않아 / 안 운동해)요.

   I don't exercise.

2 오늘 (일 안 했어 / 일하지 않았어 / 안 일했어)요.

   I didn't work today.

3 한국 음식을 (좋아 안 해 / 좋아하지 않아 / 안 좋아해)요.

   I don't like Korean food.

4 저희 할머니는 (건강 안 해 / 건강하지 않아 / 안 건강해)요.

   My grandma isn't healthy.

ANSWER
1 운동 안 해/운동하지 않아
2 일 안 했어/일하지 않았어
3 좋아하지 않아/안 좋아해
4 건강하지 않아/안 건강해

4 Verbs that are Negative by Nature

Some verbs sound unnatural when negated with **안**, because their opposites already carry a negative meaning.

The most common examples of these verbs were covered in Chapter 5, but let's bring them up again for a quick review.

Verb		Negative Verb
이다	↔	아니다 (not 안 이다)
있다	↔	없다 (not 안 있다)

> * All adjectives that end in –있다 can be negated by changing –있다 to –없다.

Verb		Negative Verb
알다	↔	모르다 (not 안 알다)
잘하다	↔	못하다 (not 안 잘하다)

e.g. I'm not a student.

√ 학생 아니에요.   x 학생 안 이에요.

I don't have kids.

√ 아이가 없어요.   x 아이가 안 있어요.

It's not fun. (=It's boring.)

√ 재미없어요.   x 안 재미있어요.

I don't know this word.

√ 이 단어 몰라요.   x 이 단어 안 알아요.

I'm not good at Korean.

√ 한국어 못해요.   x 한국어 안 잘해요.

1   **True or False**

① **안** is an adverb that can be used to negate verbs and adjectives.   ☐ / ☐
       TRUE   FALSE

② **안 울어요** and **울지 않아요** mean the same thing.   ☐ / ☐
       TRUE   FALSE

③ The correct way to negate the verb **생각하다** is **안 생각하다**.   ☐ / ☐
       TRUE   FALSE

④ The correct way to negate the adjective **친절하다** is **안 친절하다**.   ☐ / ☐
       TRUE   FALSE

⑤ The correct way to negate the verb **알다** is **안 알다**.   ☐ / ☐
       TRUE   FALSE

2   **Select one INCORRECTLY negated sentence and correct the error.**

① 저는 주말에 공부하지 않아요.

② 뜨거운 물을 마시지 않을 거예요.

③ 지금 집에 안 있어요.

④ 엄마한테 말 안 했어요.

⑤ 오늘 비가 안 왔어요.

3   **Fill in the blank with the correct negated form of the given verbs/ adjectives using 안.**

① 그 영화를 [   ]요.
     I won't watch that movie.

② 여동생한테 선물을 [   ]요.
     I didn't give the gift to my younger sister.

③ 주말에 [   ]요.
     I don't work on the weekends.

④ 저는 헬스장에서 [   ]요.
     I don't work out at the gym.

⑤ 너무 짠 음식은 [   ]요.
     Foods that are too salty aren't healthy.

4   Translate the following sentences in the –요 ending 존댓말 using –지 않다.

① My cat isn't small. [   ]

② It wasn't expensive. [   ]

③ I wasn't sick yesterday. I was tired. (피곤하다 : to be tired)

[   ]

④ I won't be busy this weekend.

[   ]

5   Write the negative version of each sentence in the –요 ending 존댓말.

① 저는 선생님이에요.   ↔   [   ]

② 오늘 날씨가 좋아요.   ↔   [   ]

③ 저는 한국어를 잘해요.   ↔   [   ]

④ 길을 알아요.   ↔   [   ]

⑤ 제 딸은 채소를 좋아해요.   ↔   [   ]

⑥ 그 사람은 친절해요.   ↔   [   ]

ANSWER

1   ① T   ② T   ③ F (It should be 생각 안 하다)   ④ T   ⑤ F (It should be 모르다)

2   ③ 안 있어요→ 없어요

3   ① 안 볼 거예   ② 안 줬어   ③ 일 안 해   ④ 운동 안 해   ⑤ 안 건강해

4   ① 제 고양이는 작지 않아요.   ② 비싸지 않았어요.   ③ 어제 아프지 않았어요. 피곤했어요.
    ④ 이번 주말에 바쁘지 않을 거예요.

5   ① 저는 선생님(이) 아니에요. (I'm not a teacher.)

    ② 오늘 날씨가 안 좋아요 (or 좋지 않아요). (The weather is not nice today.)

    ③ 저는 한국어를 못해요 (or 잘하지 않아요). (I'm not good at Korean.)

    ④ 길을 몰라요. (I don't know the way/direction.)

    ⑤ 제 딸은 채소를 안 좋아해요 (or 좋아하지 않아요). (My daughter doesn't like vegetables.)

    ⑥ 그 사람은 안 친절해요 (or 친절하지 않아요). (That person isn't kind.)

Adverbs Commonly Used with Negative Verbs

Let's learn some adverbs that are often used in negative sentences.

❶ 아직 : still, yet

아직 has two meanings: "still" and "yet." When used in a positive sentence, it means "still." In a negative sentence, it means "yet."

Positive Sentence	Negative Sentence
저는 아직 학생이에요. I'm still a student.	아직 봄이 아니에요. It's not spring yet.
물이 아직 차가워요. The water's still cold.	아직 안 배웠어요. I haven't learned it yet.
아직 배우고 있어요. I'm still learning.	아직 안 갈 거예요. I won't go yet.

When you want to emphasize that something is a lot slower than expected, you can add 도 and say 아직도.

For example, if you are really looking forward to spring and it feels like time is moving too slowly, you can say 아직도 봄이 아니에요. Or, if you've taken a long break from school and graduation keeps getting delayed, you can say 저는 아직도 학생이에요.

❷ 별로 : not really, not much

e.g. 별로 안 좋아해요. I don't really like it.

별로 맛없어요. It doesn't really taste good.

한국어를 별로 못해요. I'm not really good at Korean.

❸ 그렇게 : not that much, not very

그렇게 originally means "like that," and it's the adverb form of the adjective 그렇다 (to be like that).

You can use it like 그렇게 배웠어요 (I learned it like that) or 그렇게 생각해요? (Do you think like that?/Do you think so?).

But in negative sentences, it can mean "not that much."

e.g. 그렇게 좋아하지 않아요. I don't like it that much.

그렇게 어렵지 않아요. It's not that difficult.

그렇게 많지 않아요. There isn't that many/much.

The difference between 그렇게 and 별로 is that 그렇게 usually compares something to expectations, while 별로 doesn't directly compare it to anything and simply states your impression as is.

한국어는 별로 어렵지 않아요!
여러분도 그렇게 생각해요?

CHAPTER 13

The –ㅂ/습니다 Ending

So far, we've practiced using the –요 ending in polite speech. In this chapter, we'll focus on the –ㅂ/습니다 ending.

There are mainly two types of **존댓말** (polite language) in Korean: sentences ending with −요 and those ending with −ㅂ/습니다.

The difference between these two lies in the level of formality. Generally, −ㅂ/습니다 is considered more formal than −요.

As beginner Korean learners, you'll probably use the −요 ending more often. However, when you hear people introduce themselves in a formal setting, or even in announcements or news, you'll often hear the −ㅂ/습니다 ending.

This ending also shows up a lot in reading passages on the TOPIK[*] exam. So it would actually be useful to become familiar with both endings.

In this chapter, we'll practice making Korean sentences with the −ㅂ/습니다 ending. It's quite simple, but it does follow certain rules.

---

[*] TOPIK stands for Test of Proficiency in Korean and is an officially recognized Korean language proficiency test administered by government institutions.

1 Present Tense

| Stem | + | ㅂ/습니다 |

To the stem of the verb on adjective, you attach either ㅂ (if the stem ends in a vowel) or 습 (if the stem ends in a consonant) and then add 니다.

(1) Stem ends in a vowel

이다 (to be noun) ⟶ 입니다

아니다 (to be not noun) ⟶ 아닙니다

가다 (to go) ⟶ 갑니다

보다 (to watch) ⟶ 봅니다

비싸다 (to be expensive) ⟶ 비쌉니다

행복하다 (to be happy) ⟶ 행복합니다

(2) Stem ends in a consonant

먹다 (to eat) ⟶ 먹습니다

읽다 (to read) ⟶ 읽습니다

있다 (to be there, to have) ⟶ 있습니다

덥다 (to be hot) ⟶ 덥습니다

어렵다 (to be hard) ⟶ 어렵습니다

−지 않다 (to be not v/a) ⟶ −지 않습니다

(3) Irregular Rules

There is one group of verbs that behave irregularly when combined with the
−ㅂ/습니다 ending: verbs that end in ㄹ. For these verbs, you replace the
ㄹ with ㅂ in the stem and then add 니다.

살다 (to live) ⟶ 삽니다

놀다 (to play) ⟶ 놉니다

길다 (to be long) ⟶ 깁니다

달다 (to be sweet) ⟶ 답니다

만들다 (to make) ⟶ 만듭니다

Aside from ㄹ-ending verbs, no other group of verbs follows an irregular
pattern when used with −ㅂ/습니다 in the present tense. Even verbs that
are irregular in conjugations, such as 어렵다 (to be difficult) or 듣다 (to listen),
follow the regular pattern. Since their stems end in a consonant, you simply
add −습니다, resulting in 어렵습니다 or 듣습니다.

 연습

▶ **TRACK 47**

Now that you know how to form sentences with −ㅂ/습니다 in present
tense, fill in the blank below with the correct verb and adjective in its
−ㅂ/습니다 form.

① 저는 간호사 [⎯⎯⎯⎯⎯].

I'm a nurse.

② 이건 제 책이 [⎯⎯⎯⎯⎯].

This is not my book.

③ 저는 매일 학교에 [⎯⎯⎯⎯⎯].

I go to school every day.

④ 오늘 날씨가 너무 ☐ .

The weather is too hot today.

⑤ 요즘 정말 ☐ .

I'm really happy these days.

⑥ 강아지는 초콜릿을 ☐ .

Dogs don't eat chocolate.

⑦ 피곤하지 ☐ .

I'm not tired.

⑧ 한국어는 조금 ☐ .

Korean is a bit difficult.

⑨ 콘서트 표가 너무 ☐ .

The concert ticket is too expensive.

⑩ 아빠는 아침에 신문을 ☐ .

Dad reads the newspaper in the morning.

⑪ 질문이 ☐ .

I have a question.

⑫ 저는 큰 도시에 ☐ .

I live in a big city.

ANSWER

① 입니다 ② 아닙니다 ③ 갑니다 ④ 덥습니다
⑤ 행복합니다 ⑥ 안 먹습니다 or 먹지 않습니다
⑦ 않습니다 ⑧ 어렵습니다 ⑨ 비쌉니다
⑩ 읽습니다 (봅니다 is okay, too!) ⑪ 있습니다
⑫ 삽니다

Past Tense

┌─────────────────────────┐   ┌─────────────────────┐
│ **Present Conjugation** │ + │   ㅆ 습니다   │
└─────────────────────────┘   └─────────────────────┘

For the past tense, you add the final consonant **ㅆ** to the present tense conjugation, and then add **습니다**.

오다 (to come)
와 + ㅆ습니다 ⟶ 왔습니다

마시다 (to drink)
마셔 + ㅆ습니다 ⟶ 마셨습니다

사다 (to buy)
사 + ㅆ습니다 ⟶ 샀습니다

배우다 (to learn)
배워 + ㅆ습니다 ⟶ 배웠습니다

공부하다 (to study)
공부해 + ㅆ습니다 ⟶ 공부했습니다

닫다 (to close)
닫아 + ㅆ습니다 ⟶ 닫았습니다

없다 (to be not there, to not have)

없어 + ㅆ습니다 ⟶ 없었습니다

아름답다 (to be beautiful)

아름다워 + ㅆ습니다 ⟶ 아름다웠습니다

친절하다 (to be kind)

친절해 + ㅆ습니다 ⟶ 친절했습니다

길다 (to be long)

길어 + ㅆ습니다 ⟶ 길었습니다

 연습

⏵ **TRACK 48**

Fill in the blank below with the correct verb and adjective in its −ㅂ/습니다 form.

① 문을 [   ].

I closed the door.

② 차를 좀 [   ].

I drank some tea.

③ 동료가 오늘 회사에 안 [   ].

My coworker didn't come to work today.

④ 학교에서 한국어를 [   ].

I learned Korean at school.

⑤ 선생님께서 학교에 [   ].

The teacher wasn't at school.

⑥ 사람들이 아주 [   ].

The people were very kind.

⑦ 경치가 아주 [   ].

The view was so beautiful.

⑧ 시장에서 과일을 좀 [   ].

I bought some fruit at the market.

⑨ 줄이 너무 [   ].

The queue was too long.

⑩ 시험 공부를 하지 [   ].

I didn't study for the test.

ANSWER

① 닫았습니다 ② 마셨습니다

③ 왔습니다 ④ 배웠습니다

⑤ 없었습니다 ⑥ 친절했습니다

⑦ 아름다웠습니다 ⑧ 샀습니다

⑨ 길었습니다 ⑩ 않았습니다

3 Future Tense

V/A-ㄹ/을 것입니다
→ V/A-ㄹ/을 겁니다

We learned that the basic future tense pattern goes like this: Stem + ㄹ/을 것 + 이다.

When combining Stem + ㄹ/을 것이다 with the -ㅂ/습니다 ending, you attach ㅂ니다 (since 이다 ends with a vowel). This makes the final form Stem + ㄹ/을 것입니다.

In many cases, 것입니다 is shortened to 겁니다, becoming Stem + ㄹ/을 겁니다.

Both forms are correct, but in this book, we'll focus more on using 겁니다 instead of 것입니다.

주다 (to give)
줄 겁니다 (= 줄 것입니다)

보내다 (to send)
보낼 겁니다 (= 보낼 것입니다)

만들다 (to make)
만들 겁니다 (= 만들 것입니다)
irregular

많다 (to be many)
많을 겁니다 (= 많을 것입니다)

울다 (to cry)
울 겁니다 (= 울 것입니다)
irregular

(배가) 고프다 (to be hungry)

고플 겁니다 (= 고플 것입니다)

바쁘다 (to be busy)

바쁠 겁니다 (= 바쁠 것입니다)

작다 (to be small)

작을 겁니다 (= 작을 것입니다)

뜨겁다 (to be hot)

뜨거울 겁니다 (= 뜨거울 것입니다)
irregular

듣다 (to listen)

들을 겁니다 (= 들을 것입니다)
irregular

연습

Fill in the blank with the future tense – ㅂ니다 ending.
(Please use 겁니다 instead of 것입니다.)

① 이메일을 [＿＿＿＿＿].

    I will send an email.

② 방금 만들었습니다. 그래서 [＿＿＿＿＿].

    I just made it. So it will be hot.

③ 친구에게 [＿＿＿＿＿].

    I will give it to a friend.

④ 수업을 [＿＿＿＿＿].

    I will listen to a class. (= I will take a class.)

⑤ 저녁에 배가 [＿＿＿＿＿].

    You'll be hungry in the evening.

⑥ [＿＿＿＿＿].

    I won't cry.

⑦ 도서관에 학생들이 [＿＿＿＿＿].

    There will be many students in the library.

⑧ 이 모자는 저한테 너무 [＿＿＿＿＿].

    This hat will be too small for me.

⑨ 저희 회사는 다음 주에 [＿＿＿＿＿].

    Our company will be busy next week.

ANSWER

① 보낼 겁니다 ② 뜨거울 겁니다 ③ 줄 겁니다 ④ 들을 겁니다 ⑤ 고플 겁니다
⑥ 안 울 겁니다 / 울지 않을 겁니다 ⑦ 많을 겁니다 ⑧ 작을 겁니다 ⑨ 바쁠 겁니다

1   Select one sentence where the -ㅂ/습니다 form is used INCORRECTLY in each tense, and correct it to the proper form.

(1) Present Tense

① 저는 이 사람을 모릅니다.　② 그 강아지는 다리가 짧습니다.

③ 저는 한국 노래를 안 듣습니다.　④ 요즘 날씨가 추웁니다.

⑤ 이 초콜릿은 너무 답니다.

```
┌────────────────────────┐
│                        │
│                        │
└────────────────────────┘
```

(2) Past Tense

① 친구가 어제 많이 아팠습니다.　② 작년에 한국어를 배웠습니다.

③ 재미있는 책을 읽었습니다.　④ 친구한테 선물을 받았습니다.

⑤ 이상한 사람을 만났습니다.

```
┌────────────────────────┐
│                        │
│                        │
└────────────────────────┘
```

(3) Future Tense

① 사장님께 이메일을 보낼 겁니다.　② 이번 주에 비가 안 올 겁니다.

③ 한국어 팟캐스트를 들을 겁니다.　④ 이번 주말에 가족에게 전화할 겁니다.

⑤ 편의점이 여기에서 가깝을 겁니다.

```
┌────────────────────────┐
│                        │
│                        │
└────────────────────────┘
```

2   Translate each of the following sentences into Korean using the -ㅂ/습니다 ending.

① The train is too slow. (느리다)

_____

② The baby cries every day. (울다)

_____

③ The water is too cold. (차갑다)

_____

④ I didn't buy it yet. (사다)

_____

⑤ I will go to sleep early today. (자다, 일찍)

_____

3   Fill in the blank with –ㅂ/습니다 ending, using the words from the box.

①

많다	바쁘다	피곤하다	쉬다
to be many	to be busy	to be tired	to rest

요즘 저는 일이 [　　　]. 그래서 아주 ˢᵒ [　　　]. 하지만 ᵇᵘᵗ

어제는 너무 [　　　]. 그래서 하루 종일 ᵗʰᵉ ʷʰᵒˡᵉ ᵈᵃʸ [　　　].

These days, I have a lot of work. So I'm very busy. But yesterday, I was too tired. So I rested the whole day.

②

가다	재미없다	보다
to go	to be boring, not fun	to watch

영화관에 [　　　]. 영화가 별로 [　　　].

다음에는 무서운 ˢᶜᵃʳʸ 영화를 [　　　].

I went to the movie theater. The movie wasn't very fun. Next time, I won't watch scary movies.

③

살다	귀엽다	많다	치우다
to live	to be cute	to be many	to clean up

저는 고양이와 강아지랑 [   ]. 아주 [   ]. 하지만

집에 털이^fur [   ]. 그래서 매일 집을 [   ].

I live with a cat and a dog. They are so cute. But there is a lot of fur in the house. So I clean up the house every day.

④

잘하다	가르치다	배우다	늘다
to be good at	to teach	to learn	to improve

저는 영어를 [   ]. 그래서 어린^young 아이들에게 영어를

[   ]. 제 수업에서 단어와 문법을 많이 [   ].

아이들의 영어가 많이 [   ].

I speak good English. So I teach English to young kids. They learn a lot of words and grammar in my class. Their English has improved a lot.

⑤

이다	오다	주다	많다	먹다	있다
to be	to come	to give	to be many	to eat	to be there

오늘은 제 생일 ⬚. 친구들이 저희 집에

⬚. 저에게 생일 선물로 큰 상자^{box}를 ⬚.

안에 과자^{snacks}가 ⬚. 저희는 맛있는 케이크를 같이

⬚. 재미있는 하루 ⬚.

Today is my birthday. My friends came to my house. They gave me a big box as a birthday gift. There were many snacks inside. We ate a delicious cake together. It was a fun day.

ANSWER

1 (1) ④ 추웁니다 → 춥습니다
   ① I don't know this person.
   ② That dog has short legs.
   ③ I don't listen to Korean songs.
   ④ These days, the weather is cold.
   ⑤ This chocolate is too sweet.

   (2) ② 배웠습니다 → 배웠습니다
   ① My friend was very sick yesterday.
   ② I learned Korean last year.
   ③ I read a good/fun book.
   ④ I received a gift from a friend.
   ⑤ I met a strange person.

   (3) ⑤ 가깝을 겁니다 → 가까울 겁니다
   ① I will email my boss.
   ② It won't rain this week.
   ③ I will listen to a Korean podcast.
   ④ I will call my family this weekend.
   ⑤ The convenience store will be close from here.

2 ① 기차가 너무 느립니다. ② 아기가 매일 웁니다. ③ 물이 너무 차갑습니다.
   ④ 아직 안 샀습니다 (사지 않았습니다) ⑤ 오늘 일찍 잘 겁니다.

3 ① 많습니다, 바쁩니다, 피곤했습니다, 쉬었습니다
   ② 갔습니다, 재미없었습니다, 안 볼 겁니다(보지 않을 겁니다)
   ③ 삽니다, 귀엽습니다, 많습니다, 치웁니다
   ④ 잘합니다, 가르칩니다, 배웁니다, 늘었습니다
   ⑤ 입니다, 왔습니다, 줬습니다, 많았습니다, 먹었습니다, 였습니다

What does 좀 really mean?

Listening to Korean conversations, you've probably heard 좀 a lot. 좀 is actually a shortened form of 조금, which means "a little" or "a bit." But unlike 조금, 좀 is used in various ways beyond its literal meaning.

❶ When Asking for Requests or Favors

좀 is often used to soften a request or favor.

> *e.g.* 물 좀 주세요. Water, please.
>
> 설탕 좀. Sugar, please. (반말)
>
> 조용히 좀 해주세요. Please be quiet.

But just to clarify, 좀 isn't used when making a monetary order. For instance, at a café, we typically say 커피 주세요 to order coffee. If you say 커피 좀 주세요, it sounds more like "pass me the coffee."

❷ Some

좀 can also mean "some," indicating a reasonable amount.

> *e.g.* 물 좀 마셨어요. I had some water.
>
> 옷 좀 샀어요. I bought some clothes.

❸ Filler Word

좀 is often used as a filler word while you think of what to say next. It works similarly to "like" in English.

> *e.g.* A 맛이 어때요? How does it taste?
>
> B 좀… 쓰지만 달아요. It's like… bitter but sweet.

Appendix

Personal Pronouns in Korean

We've learned the Korean words for "I" and "You," but you may have noticed that "You," "He," "She," and "They" don't have a single universal equivalent in Korean. Unlike many other languages, Korean doesn't use fixed pronouns for these words in every context. In this appendix, we'll explore how personal pronouns work in Korean and the different ways they are used.

Personal pronouns in Korean work quite differently
from English. Except for "I" and "We,"
there isn't a direct equivalent for "You," "He," "She,"
and "They." While we do have those pronouns,
they are rarely used in daily conversation,
making them not very practical. Instead,
many alternative words are used to express each of
those pronouns.

In this chapter, we'll explore different alternatives for
"You," "He," "She," and "They," focusing on the most
commonly used ones. Along the way, you'll also pick up
new basic vocabulary and gain insights into aspects of
Korean culture. Rather than approaching this chapter
with the pressure to remember everything, feel free to
think of it as reading for fun!

1 You

Let's first explore different ways to express "You" in Korean.

In Korean, the only direct equivalent for "You" is 너.

However, 너 is 반말 (casual language), so using it in polite expressions would be inappropriate and sound rude. Even when it's used in casual language, it can still be inappropriate depending on who it is you're speaking to.

Now let's learn proper and diverse ways to say "you" in both polite and causal language.

1. "You" in 존댓말 (Polite Language)

There isn't a single designated word for "you" in 존댓말, and there are many different ways to say "You." Let's explore some of the most common ones.

(1) Completely omit "you"

As we learned in the previous chapter, in Korean, it's quite common to omit the subject in a sentence when the situation or context makes it obvious.

For instance, if it's evident that you're talking about yourself, omitting "I" is acceptable. Similarly, when discussing or questioning someone else while facing them, it's usually implied that the conversation is directed at them. So it's natural to omit "You" because the context makes it clear.

While omitting "You" in your sentence is the most convenient way, there are instances where including "You" becomes essential, and doing so can foster a slightly more friendly connection. Therefore, it's beneficial to learn alternative words to use for "You" in those cases.

(2) First name + 씨 or First name + 님

One way is using the other person's first name, but, of course, it's not just the name; you should add **씨** or **님** after the name.

Both **씨** and **님** are titles conveying respect and politeness, but they are slightly different.

❶ **Name + 씨** : **씨** is used to address someone with a respectful tone without being overly formal. It is commonly used with colleagues of a similar age, younger coworkers, or adult classmates.

❷ **Name + 님** : **님** is a more polite and formal expression than **씨**. It is appropriate when addressing individuals who require extra courtesy, such as customers, someone significantly older than you, or someone you are meeting for the first time.

Short Dialogue ▶ **TRACK 50**

지수 씨 정말 똑똑해요.
You are so smart.

규진 씨도 똑똑해요.
You are smart, too.

규진   지수

(3) In professional settings

You can address someone by their job title in a workplace or their profession.

❶ Job Title + 님

Korean companies have various job titles, which may vary slightly depending on the company. But they typically follow a hierarchy, starting from the lower ranks and progressing upwards, such as **사원** (Employee), **주임** (Assistant Manager), **대리** (Deputy Manager), **과장** (Manager), **차장** (Deputy General Manager), **부장** (General Manager), **사장** (President), and **회장** (Chairman).

For example, if I hold the title of **대리** (Deputy Manager) at a company and I'm speaking with a **과장** (Manager), I would address them as **과장님**, while they would address me as **대리님**. In many cases, you can also add their surname, such as **김 대리님** or **박 과장님**, for added specificity.

In smaller companies, the CEO or founder is often addressed as **대표**. So, when speaking with the founder of the company you work for, you would call them **대표님**.

❷ Profession + 님/선생님

You can also address someone by adding **님** or **선생님** to their profession.

While **선생님** means "teacher," it doesn't always refer to someone who is actually a teacher. It's often used as a polite way to address someone.

For example, if someone's job is a lawyer (**변호사**), people might address them as **변호사님** or 변호사 선생님. They could also include the person's surname, like **윤 변호사님**, to be more specific.

Similarly, when addressing doctors (**의사**), it's more common to say **의사 선생님** rather than **의사님**.

One interesting fact about the word 선생님 is that, in Korean, the lack of a direct equivalent for "you" can make addressing strangers tricky. In such cases, 선생님 is a common alternative.

For example, I once received a call from a librarian because I had an overdue book, and they addressed me as 선생님. It wasn't because they knew my profession was a teacher, but because 선생님 is often used to address someone when you don't know what else to call them, while maintaining a tone of respect.

But of course, it's not the only option, and the choice of word can vary depending on the setting. For example, in a store, it's much more common for a staff to address customers as 손님 or 고객님, which both mean "customer."

(4) In school settings

In school settings, it's common to use 반말 with your peers or classmates. But when it comes to addressing teachers, professors, seniors, or even classmates whom you are not very close or acquainted with, there are polite ways to call them "You."

Firstly, you can address your teachers as "you" using 선생님.

In university or college setting, you can address your professors as "you" using 교수님 (professor).

Professors can call their students "you" using "Name + 학생 (student)."

Short Dialogue ⊙ **TRACK 51**

지수 학생 잘 지내요?
Are you doing well?

네.
교수님도 잘 지내세요?
Yes. Are you doing well yourself?

교수님   지수

Then how about addressing your fellow students?

You can call those who began school before you 선배 (senior) + 님,
and those who started school after you 후배 (junior) + 님.
If someone is neither a senior nor a junior but simply a student studying together
or a classmate in the same school, you can address them as 학우님. If you're
somewhat close to that particular classmate or don't want to sound too distant, you
can use **First Name** + 씨.

* 학우: fellow student, school peer

(5) If you don't know their name or job…

In this case, the safest and simplest way to say "You" is by calling them 선생님.

There are more ways, of course. You can call them **남자분**, **여자분**, **사장님** or
사모님 as well.

남자 means "a man/male" and **여자** means "a woman/female." **분** means "person"
and it's an honorific word that adds more respect to the person being addressed.
님 is usually attached after a person's distinct name, job, or title. Therefore, in this
context, using **분** instead of **님** sounds more natural.

사장님 means a president of a company, but beyond its literal meaning, it is also used
respectfully to address anyone you are not acquainted with. It can be used for both
males and females. There is also **사모님**, which is a female version of **사장님** and can
be used for females only.

You can think of **사장님** and **사모님** as similar to addressing someone as "Sir"
or "Madam/Ma'am" in English.

 꿀팁

How about 아저씨 and 아주머니?

아저씨 is a word used for middle-aged[*] men, and 아주머니 for middle-
aged women. (While 아줌마 is another term, it can sound quite offensive, so
people often opt for 아주머니 to sound politer.)

Although both 아저씨 and 아주머니 are common, it's recommended to be a bit careful when using these words, because in some cases, calling someone 아저씨 or 아주머니 might unintentionally make them seem a bit older than they actually are.

> * The perception of "middle-aged" can vary depending on cultural and social contexts, so there isn't an exact age range that corresponds to 아저씨 or 아주머니. For example, to a young child, any adult man might seem old, so they might call a man in his mid-20s 아저씨. Meanwhile, some people consider any married man over 30 to be an 아저씨. Although there's no fixed age for these words, keep in mind that they do carry a slightly "older" connotation.

How about 당신?

If you search for the Korean word for "you" in a translator or dictionary, it will most likely show up as 당신. However, 당신 is rarely used in daily conversation and is mostly found in formal or written contexts. It is also commonly used in sentimental or emotional writings, such as poetry or song lyrics. (그대 is another word for "you" that is often used in poetry or song lyrics.)

If 당신 is used in everyday conversations, it typically falls into one of the following scenarios:

❶ Between spouses: Married couples may address each other as 당신, which can be somewhat similar to terms like "dear" or "honey." Interestingly, it is more commonly used among the older generation, while younger couples tend to avoid it. Among the younger generation, 여보 is more often used as "dear" or "honey."

❷ During arguments: If two people, not necessarily a couple, refer to each other as 당신 during a disagreement, it signals a high likelihood of tension or conflict. This indicates that referring to someone as 당신 can be seen as impolite and aggressive, and it's advisable to avoid addressing the other person as 당신, even in heated situations.

2. "You" in 반말 (Casual Language)

As we learned, "You" in 반말 is 너.

However, you shouldn't address everyone you're close with as 너. 너 is typically used only for those who are the same age or younger, and very rarely for those who are older even if you are close.

This is deeply related to Korea's age culture. Korean culture tends to place significant importance on age, and even if someone is only a year or two older, it's rare to address them as 너, no matter how close you are. Of course you can still use 반말 with them, but you cannot call them 너.

Then, how would you address your close but older friends or family members as "you?"

In Korean, there are many specific terms for addressing individuals based on their age and relationship. Let's learn some of the most common ones that are derived from family context.

When you're close to someone older, it's common to address them as 형/오빠 (older male) or 누나/언니 (older female).

형 and 오빠 originally mean "older brother" in a family context, while 누나 and 언니 mean "older sister." You can not only use them for your older siblings but also your older friends.

Keep in mind that you can call someone 형 or 누나 only if you are male, and 오빠 or 언니 only if you are female.

For example, I am the middle child of three siblings. Since I'm a girl, I call my older sister 언니, and my younger brother calls me 누나.

When addressing your parents or grandparents, who are undoubtedly older than you, it's obvious that you should never use 너.

You can simply address your parents as 엄마 (mom) or 아빠 (dad).

For grandparents, you can use 할머니 (grandmother) or 할아버지 (grandfather).

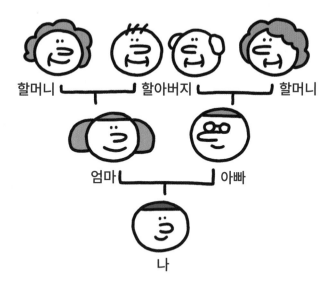

 In a Nutshell

You in 반말	If the speaker is male	If the speaker is female
Same age or younger	너	
Older Male	형	오빠
Older Female	누나	언니
Mom	엄마	
Dad	아빠	
Grandmother	할머니	
Grandfather	할아버지	

*All these words, except 너, can also be used in polite speech (존댓말). For example, you might address an older female as 누나 or 언니, but if they haven't permitted you to use casual speech (반말), you'd still speak politely (존댓말) while calling them that. Similarly, some people use 반말 with their grandparents, while others use 존댓말. So rather than taking these words as exclusively casual (반말) forms of "you," it's better to think of them as common terms for "you" in casual contexts.

Quiz

Fill in the blank with the word that corresponds to "You" according to context.

(Don't worry too much about understanding every part of the example sentences. Just focus on the appropriate pronouns for "You.")

1   You want to tell your <u>younger sibling</u> "You have to wake up early."

      [   ] 일찍 일어나야 돼.

2   You want to tell your <u>older male friend</u> "You look happy."

      [   ] 행복해 보여.

3   You want to tell your <u>older sister</u> "You are so funny."

      [   ] 너무 웃겨.

4   You want to tell your <u>mom</u> "You work too hard."

      [   ] 너무 열심히 일해.

5   You want to tell your <u>grandmother</u> "You cook so well."

      [   ] 요리 너무 잘해.

ANSWER

1 너   2 형/오빠   3 누나/언니
4 엄마   5 할머니

3. What about Plural "You?"

Then what if you want to say plural "You" as in "You guys" or "You people?"

(1) Add 들 after the singular "you"

–들 makes a specific noun plural.

For example, if you want to address several teachers, you can say **선생님들**.

If you want to address several men, you can say **남자분들** or **사장님들**. Likewise, if you want to address several women, you can say **여자분들**, **사장님들**, or **사모님들**.

It's the same in **반말**.

When you want to address several older female friends, you can say **누나들/언니들**, and when addressing several older male friends, you can say **형들/오빠들**.

(2) Unique plural form of 너 (You)

However, when using **너** to address people of the same age or younger, **너들** is not the correct form.

너희 or **너네** is the correct plural form.

너희 and **너네** are already plural, but it's also okay to add **들** and say **너희들** and **너네들**.

(3) When gender and age vary

When addressing a group of people with different ages or genders, there are several options you can use, with the most common one being **여러분**.

I also use **여러분** in my videos to address my audience/students. You've probably also heard other YouTubers or celebrities use **여러분** frequently.

Other alternatives include **다(들)** and **모두(들)**. While **다** and **모두** mean "everything," they can also be used to refer to "everyone" when talking about people. Although **다** and **모두** inherently carry a plural meaning, adding extra **들** is also common.

Example Scenarios

· A speaker addressing a large crowd

여러분께서 참석해주셔서 정말 기쁩니다. I'm happy that you all came.

· A teacher addressing young students

너희들 숙제 다 했어? Did you guys finish the homework?

· When calling women you don't know the name of

여자분들 괜찮으세요? Are you okay?

· When calling older male friends

형들(or 오빠들) 뭐 해? What are you doing?

· When addressing friends of the same age or younger

너네 배고파? Are you hungry?

 In a Nutshell

Plural "You"	존댓말	반말
Adding 들 after a singular form	e.g. 선생님들, 남자분들, 여자분들, 사장님들, 사모님들 etc	누나들, 언니들, 형들, 오빠들 etc
너's unique plural form		너희(들), 너네(들)
When gender and age vary	여러분 다(들), 모두(들)	

2 He, She, and They

Just like "You," there is no one-to-one equivalent for "He," "She," and "They" in Korean; it depends on who you're referring to, the relationship, and the level of respect you want to express. Just like "You," it can also be omitted if it's obvious who you are talking about.

If you look it up in a dictionary, he, she, and they will likely appear as 그, 그녀, and 그들. However, these words are rarely used in daily conversations and can sound overly formal or even poetic if you use them.

The nouns corresponding to alternative pronouns for "You" can also be used for "He" and "She." In fact, there are many more alternative words for "He, She, They" compared to those for "You." This is because the person being referred to could be nearby, not here at all, or even far away. In such cases, we can use the different modifiers we've learned, like 이, 그, and 저, in each situation.

With that said, here are some of the most common ones :

1. He

이 사람 (literally, this person)

그 사람 (literally, that person)

저 사람 (literally, that person over there)

이 분 (literally, this person, but in a more respectful way)

그 분 (literally, that person, but in a more respectful way)

저 분 (literally, that person over there, but in a more respectful way)

이 남자 (literally, this man)

그 남자 (literally, that man)

저 남자 (literally, that man over there)

이 남자분 (literally, this man, but in a more respectful way)

그 남자분 (literally, that man, but in a more respectful way)

저 남자분 (literally, that man over there, but in a more respectful way)

이 남자애 * (literally, this boy)

그 남자애 (literally, that boy)

저 남자애 (literally, that boy over there)

*The word 애 is a shortened form of 아이, which means "child" or "kid."

There are also other pronouns that include **애**, commonly used in **반말**.
While **애** primarily means "kid," it's not exclusively used to refer to young children.
It can also be used for someone the same age as you or younger.

얘 (short for **이 애**,
which literally means "this person
[who is the same age as me or younger.]")

걔 (short for **그 애**,
which literally means "that person
[who is the same age as me or younger.]")

쟤 (short for **저 애**,
which literally means "that person over there
[who is the same age as me or younger.])

Using **얘**, **걔** and **쟤** for someone older or not close to you is considered rude,
so be careful to use it only for someone you are familiar with and is the same
age or younger.

2. She

이 사람 (literally, this person)

그 사람 (literally, that person)

저 사람 (literally, that person over there)

이 분 (literally, this person, but in a more respectful way)

그 분 (literally, that person, but in a more respectful way)

저 분 (literally, that person over there, but in a more respectful way)

이 여자 (literally, this woman)

그 여자 (literally, that woman)

저 여자 (literally, that woman over there)

이 여자분 (literally, this woman, but in a more respectful way)

그 여자분 (literally, that woman, but in a more respectful way)

저 여자분 (literally, that woman over there, but in a more respectful way)

이 여자애 (literally, this girl)

그 여자애 (literally, that girl)

저 여자애 (literally, that girl over there)

얘 (short for 이 애)

걔 (short for 그 애)

쟤 (short for 저 애)

3. They

You can simply put −들 after the singular person noun.

이 사람들 (literally, these people)

그 분들 (literally, those people, but in a more respectful way)

이 남자들 (literally, these men)

그 남자분들 (literally, those men, but in a more respectful way)

저 남자애들 (literally, those boys over there)

저 여자들 (literally, those women over there)

그 여자분들 (literally, those women, but in a more respectful way)

그 여자애들 (literally, those girls)

얘들 (or **얘네들**[*]) (literally, these guys)

걔들 (or **걔네들**) (literally, those guys)

쟤들 (or **쟤네들**) (literally, those guys over there)

* -네들 is a unique plural from for 너, 얘, 걔 and 쟤.

Closing Message

여러분, you've worked so hard to finish this book.
Great job, and congratulations!

수고 많았어요!

Thank you so much for choosing this book.
I hope you continue your Korean learning journey,
and that my upcoming books and
YouTube videos bring even more value
to your learning experience.

Note: The phrase 수고 많았어요
literally means "You've put in a lot of effort
and hard work." It's a common way to express
appreciation and acknowledge
someone's dedication or a job well done.
It's often used to offer warm
encouragement after completing
something challenging.